MW00577142

I wake up every morning...

looking
to help
my friends
succeed...

and some of them just happen to be clients.

Give to Grow
by Mo Bunnell

Table of Contents

Section One: **The Truth**

Section Two: **The Lies**

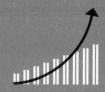

Invest in Relationships to Build Your Business and Your Career

Section Three: **The Gifts**

Section Four: **The Impact**

Section One:
The Truth

Chapter 1

When I Realized Relationships Are the Key

It wasn't normal for me to come into the office with nothing to do, but there I was, staring at the wall, feeling both anxiety and adventure. With all my tasks transitioned to my old teammates the week before, I didn't feel crunched for time like I did most mornings, wondering how everything would get done. Time was ticking so slowly I couldn't help but notice every detail in front of me: an empty office, a computer with no emails, and a Diet Mountain Dew poured over ice. The office was so quiet the soda's fizzing sounded like thunder.

"Well, good morning," my new boss said, somehow magically appearing in the doorway sipping coffee. Even though I was startled, I also was happy we could finally get started. We chitchatted about the weekend, with him trying to be nice and me trying not to show my nerves.

I'd spent most of the last eight years working as an actuary. Don't know what an actuary is? It's an applied statistician that projects insanely complex long- and short-term liabilities like pension plans and health care expenses—*super* detailed quant work. I loved it! And just a few weeks before, I had completed the last of the twenty-four exams I needed to reach the profession's highest designation, a Fellow of the Society of Actuaries.

I was an expert in what I now call Doing the Work. I knew how to build complicated models and answer my client's complex questions. I knew my stuff and knew my clients, having gotten great at delivering on relatively narrow, already-purchased projects. I hit high standards of client satisfaction externally and billable hours internally.

But now everything was different. My new role had new responsibilities, combining my comfort of Doing the Work with something very uncomfortable: *Winning* the Work.

The changes were immense and intimidating. I still had to keep clients happy and hit billable time goals, but now I also had to add so much more. I used to focus on knowing a lot about a few offerings, but now I needed to talk through hundreds of them. I used to know much more about the topic being discussed than my clients, but now they would know much more than me. I used to deliver on projects my clients purchased, but now I'd need to create the demand for my firm's solutions.

And to top it all off, most of the clients I'd be interacting with were at least twenty years older than me, some more than thirty.

I'm sure my firm had a reasonable time frame for me to learn all this, but back then, I put too much pressure on myself, expecting to master all these skills right away. As the weekend recap with my new boss died down, I awkwardly blurted out what I wanted the most that morning: "Hey, when do I get the manual on business development?"

He chuckled and I waited, thinking he was going to tell me about the firm's training programs or great books that had helped him.

What he shared next, I'll never forget. "Just do one thing. Treat the client right." I'm not sure what happened after that as fear stole my focus. At some point, he turned and left my office.

Looking back decades later, he was right. Here's what I'd now say to my younger self:

Relationships are the foundation of long-term business success.

At First, I Got in My Own Way

My early days in the new position were rough and my results rocky. I was nervous in front of clients, fearing I wouldn't know answers to their questions. I gravitated to lower-level relationships, feeling more comfortable with those closer to my age. I hesitated to follow up with clients, afraid I'd be nagging. And I assumed others were "born with it," as much of what I was trying to do seemed mysterious.

Thankfully, I had a catalyst for growth: a top-performing mentor. Together, we managed double a normal client load, splitting the responsibilities on a day-to-day basis. I couldn't have done it without him. He pushed me beyond my comfort zone, giving me goals every morning, then checking in each evening, providing an accountability hook. Knowing he'd ask "How'd it go?" that night kept me moving forward every day.

He accelerated my learning, but as I blasted through one mental barrier, I slammed into another. Each time I did, he'd tell me what to do, move by move, often modeling how to do it himself. Even with this, I was afraid of doing something wrong, worrying about every detail in an email or conversation. Things were moving fast, yet it felt like I was moving slow.

When we won work, I'd get busy and worry about getting it all done. It was hard to deliver on what our clients bought, let alone find time to think about what they should buy next. And even if I somehow managed to invest in client relationships, I felt fragile, always worrying about looking bad, fearing I'd say something that exposed my lack of experience or not have an answer at all.

One instance really stands out because it nearly gave me an anxiety attack. After hundreds of hours invested in Winning the Work, we won—and it was the largest consulting project in our office that year. I felt the full thrill of the win that day and celebrated with my wife that night. By the end of the pursuit, I knew a few of the key clients personally and wanted to make them look great. I was all in for them, excited about spending every second in the coming months delivering on all our promises. Or so I thought.

I got in extra early the next morning to set up a war room in our largest conference space, spreading papers and plans across a huge circular table, pushing to accomplish a week's work in the first few days. The client had taken extra time to make their decision, but our timelines were the same. As I stood up so I could see the entire plan, everything felt compressed, including my comfort. There was no buffer. As I wondered how we'd hit the first milestone, my mentor raced in, clearly signaling there wasn't much time to share something important.

"I've been thinking," he said. "We should have added more scope to this project." He went on to describe four major areas the client might need help with, directing me to go talk to each of the corresponding four internal practice leaders and ask what they could do as a fixed-fee pilot project. The kicker? He made it my job to figure that all out and pitch the ideas to the Chief Human Resource Officer by the end of the day.

I thought this was a horrible idea. And I mean *horrible*.

I didn't know a thing about any of these disciplines. How would I talk about them? How would I even fit this in with everything else I had to do? Worst yet, I was deeply afraid I'd permanently damage my young relationship with the CHRO by coming across as too salesy right after they chose us for the engagement. I barely knew her!

I felt all this at once. Frozen, I couldn't speak a word to argue against the idea. My mentor got up and said, "Well, this is important to do soon. So just figure this out and call her by the end of the day. I'll check in tonight to see how it went." He left and I just stared out the window, my future now hitched to this impossible task.

The Power of Gifts

Driven by the desire to please, I started making the internal calls right away. Every expert was excited to talk to me because the word about the big win had spread, and they wanted to be involved. Because we gave each of them a relatively small, fixed dollar amount to stick to, it was easy for them to rough out a scope and outcome. The best news was that each of them wanted to start the relationship off with a bang, so they added at least double the value of what they'd normally do for that price.

All that good news brought equally bad news: I had everything I needed to call the CHRO by mid-morning, but I just couldn't do it. I kept myself busy with other tasks through a late lunch. As my end-of-day deadline loomed, I finally mustered the courage to call, slowly dialing each digit. Her assistant picked up right away. My voice shook as I asked for the CHRO and said, "I have some quick questions for her." I thought she'd triage, asking for more information, but instead of giving me a chance to explain, she said, "Oh sure, Mo! I'll run and pull her out of her meeting!"

"Oh no! That's OK. It's…" I started to say, tailing off when I heard the phone hit her desk. I was doomed. I was pulling her from a huge meeting to upsell her on things she doesn't want, right when she doesn't want to talk to me. I would have hung up, but they knew it was me. The seconds felt like hours.

The CHRO picked up the phone. "Mo?" she asked, sounding half curious and half perturbed. I had been so nervous about the call I had handwritten exactly what I'd say, so I read the opening to my script, feeling like a low-end telemarketer dialing for dollars. But I felt her lean in, saying, "OK, tell me more." I pitched the first idea, and I was shocked: she liked it. She liked the second one too. And the third as well, telling me they were just talking about that concept and worried they were behind their competition. She even loved the fourth idea. As we ended the call, she thanked me for having their back and being so proactive. She *thanked* me!

I hung up, exhausted, feeling like I had just run a road race full tilt. The whole call had lasted maybe five minutes. I stared out the window again in disbelief. Slowly shaking my head, I asked myself, "How could I have been so wrong?"

What I see now is that we were providing her with gifts—future possibilities she didn't have before that call.

I had missed two things:

1. **Giving is the fastest way to build relationships.**
2. **No matter what is happening, it's always your move to give in a meaningful way.**

Something changed in me that day. Before that, I had been motivated by *not* failing, not having to ask for my old actuarial job back. This was the first time I remember thinking I could actually succeed. My biggest insight was that there was a lot more I didn't know about winning work, so I went back to the one move I knew best from passing all those actuarial exams—I studied.

I established more and deeper mentoring relationships, preparing for and debriefing every move and meeting we were in. I led client meetings all day, orchestrated enjoyable dinners, and stayed up in hotel rooms reading books till 1 a.m. I experimented on myself, feeling both the failures and the forward movement because my name was on the line. I started taking notes, pulling my learnings together with the long-term goal of creating a comprehensive system. Trial by trial, I figured out what worked. The playbook I'd originally wanted on that first day began to emerge.

Why I Work So Hard: The Impact

Within a few fast-paced years, I was leading a couple of our largest global client relationships and having a great time doing it. One of my favorite days was when I got an excited phone call from one of our clients sharing that she had just received a big C-level promotion. I was so excited for her. We had some meetings the next week, so we made plans to have dinner to celebrate. As we clinked glasses at dinner, she stopped me cold, saying, "You know, this is because of the great work our teams have done together."

She had called me her "secret weapon" before, but this was deeper. I knew she had a special-needs child, but I didn't realize how much this promotion meant for her or how it would allow her to impact her family and workplace in new ways. I felt immense pride that our team had helped her unlock this new level of impact. Something unlocked in me, too. I had been motivated to help her and her teams succeed before, but I hadn't realized how our work would ripple far beyond those immediately involved.

I had missed another important truth:

Many people think getting great at growth is about making themselves successful, but a deeper meaning comes from making *others* successful.

As I floated back to my hotel room that night, I realized I wanted to teach other people to have a similar experience. It took a few more years to get the guts to start my own firm teaching these skills, finally starting Bunnell Idea Group in early 2006. And those notes I'd started taking years before? I still take them, capturing anything I run across, from groundbreaking scientific studies to small ideas to streamline our systems.

Now my team and I get to train and coach the highest-level professionals at the most prestigious organizations in the world, including the very best in every professional service firm sector there is: consultants, accountants, lawyers, investment bankers, architects, brokers, engineers, agency leaders, and yes, actuaries. We get to work with salespeople and account executives at the largest, most complex service-based companies. We've trained development officers and boards of global nonprofits. And the list goes on into areas most don't expect: Entrepreneurs. Speakers bureaus. Internet influencers. Authors. Recruiters. And even *internal* functional leaders in HR, IT, finance, and (gasp!) procurement. One of my personal favorite moments was training hundreds of the most senior art experts at a top auction house, where I got to sit with their CFO and witness a Giacometti sculpture sell in a frenzied auction for over $100 million.

I pinch myself that I get to do what I do. All in all, we've worked with hundreds of organizations and trained tens of thousands of professionals from every major country on the planet. Are you someone with an expertise who's looking to make a difference? Then this book is for you.

I guess I'm the typical accidental entrepreneur, because the playbook I originally wrote for myself became a business. Countless professionals want to build a business with a relationship focus like I did. The programs we've built have evolved over the decades to become a holistic system for growth. I'm proud of our facilitator-led GrowBIG trainings and my first book, *The Snowball System*. They're comprehensive, teaching every skill needed to be great at growth, with hundreds of scientific studies backing up the steps to success.

But over the years, I realized something kept coming up in our live sessions that we hadn't covered explicitly enough: mindset. That's where *Give to Grow* comes in, showing the mindset and moves that lead to success.

I'm thankful that I had the gift of struggle. My low point became a high point for me, much higher than I could have ever expected. And now I get to show you what you need to succeed and make the impact you want to make.

Chapter 2

Why This Book Is for You and Your Teams

Looking back, I feel lucky. The order, pace, pressure, and overall extreme nature of my experiences gives me a perspective few get. I'll bet you don't know many actuaries. And how many of them got thrown into a senior production role the month they finished their exams? And how many of them started a business development training company? We don't need a Monte Carlo simulation to know the odds are slim.

Here are my top learnings on why focusing on Doing the Work and Winning the Work should be your highest priority.

Doing the work made you even better at Doing the Work.

But at some point, you shift like I did, going from executing on narrow, miles-deep work to leading complex client relationships. It looks different for different roles, but the emotions are the same: scary, stirring, and... exciting. Maybe you got promoted to account executive or client relationship leader.

Maybe you got elected to partnership. Or maybe you promoted yourself to start your own business.

Some parts of the new role are the same, though: client deadlines, urgent requests, and changes keeping you up till midnight.

At some point, you have to Do the Work *and* Win the Work.

You have to keep your current relationships rocking and meet new decision-makers. You have to deliver on the work you have and expand into new functions, geographic areas, and lines of businesses. You have to stay abreast of the news in the areas you work now and in all the new areas where they might need your help.

And that's not all. The new internal responsibilities are sometimes even harder! Your internal colleagues want to get introduced to your relationships. Your leadership wants updates on your pipeline. Your client team needs more advice than ever.

Everything's an *and*. You're managing from the middle, internally, and externally, barely keeping up, and you can never seem to get to the proactive stuff. This is the shift. It's hard, but everyone who's made a big impact has made it through, and you can too.

Winning the Work is a learnable skill.

Every complex skill is both learned and earned. No one is "born with it." We've had countless professionals enter our trainings saying things like "I can't do it like Kristy does" or "I'm just not good at this." But once we start breaking it down into simple steps, they realize they can. And if they're already good, they can become great.

You can learn Winning the Work just like you can learn Doing the Work. You can create systems for the Winning just like you do for the Doing, making it predictable, repeatable, and enjoyable.

The biggest predictor of success is relationships.

Maybe that's why pure "sales" books or training classes don't feel quite right. They treat getting the deal done as the top priority, usually without mentioning relationships at all. Get the contract signed and move onto the next one. See you later, sucker!

Many even have elements of manipulation implied or explicitly covered. Just writing that sentence makes me want to take a shower. We'll take the opposite approach. We'll cover how to Win the Work, because you can only make an outsized impact when people pay you, but we'll always cover these concepts within the context of deepening and broadening the long-term relationship.

The Top Performers focus on long-term relationships, always creating wins for everyone involved. And focusing on wins for everyone is what transforms Winning the Work from something to dread to something that's fun.

Accumulating knowledge and skills matter, but your relationships will determine your ultimate success and ceiling.

Winning the Work needs to be your top priority.

Winning the Work and Doing the Work is hard at first, but like anything, it gets easier the more you do it. Getting great at growth is where you'll have the biggest impact on your career and on others. And because you have to pick one to prioritize, choose Winning the Work.

From your side, focusing on Doing the Work won't make you better at winning it, but focusing on Winning the Work will make you better at both. You'll be out there more, noticing important themes in the market-place. You'll see the "trend in spend." You'll be meeting new people to broaden and strengthen your network. And you'll be learning, getting insights on what clients are thinking, wanting, and needing.

From the client side, it's very hard to tell who's technically a better professional, but it's easy to tell who they like and want to work with. So, getting better at your Winning the Work skills differentiates you and helps you win more often, and Winning more enhances your Doing the Work skills because you're Doing more.

Mastering both the Winning and the Doing puts you in charge of your career. People that bring in business move up faster in every profession, even surpassing those more technically competent. They get to choose the work they want to do with the clients they want to work with. And the best talent follows the person bringing in business because they want to be on a winning team.

The personal impact is immense, but it's even stronger with clients. Those that master Winning the Work make an outsized impact. They create positive change, a value far beyond just Doing the Work.

Getting great at Winning the Work and Doing the Work helps you, your teams, and your clients achieve more than anyone can comprehend.

And, if there's anything I hope you take from my learnings, it's that all these skills are learnable.

How This Book Will Help You and Your Teams

Every profession has systems for learning how to Do the Work with excellence: degrees, designations, training classes, mentoring, and heck, just doing the work makes you better at Doing the Work.

But it's rare to teach Winning the Work. And when something does exist, it's usually too little or doesn't feel right. Too little looks like the forty-five-minute fireside chat at the big annual meeting or the five-minute "big win" debrief shoehorned into the monthly call. Or someone in your doorway summarizing a lifetime of learnings with "treat the client right."

Not feeling right looks like training on how to "close the deal" as if a short-term contract is more important than a lifetime relationship. Relationships are rarely mentioned in "sales training," and if they are, it's how to manipulate people like you're a used car salesperson. What can I do to put you in a car today? Nothing. Ick. Time to leave. Selling is repelling.

But focusing on growth *does* help clients. Great growth activities are things you do *for* someone, not to someone. It helps them see a positive future. It helps them know what to do. Your help unlocks their next level of success.

And, if you design the experience right, it's a joy. We can reconcile the two perspectives with this:

Your clients hate to be sold to, but they love to buy.

And that's the best news of all. You can design a great buying process, one your clients will love and one that scales. If you have one foot in Doing the Work and the other foot in Winning the Work, you deserve a system for success too.

This gets even more valuable as you scale up to a team or entire organization. The largest, most valuable work takes teams. Multifunctional teams. Or teams across geographies. Or just a *lot* of people. These are the larger efforts, the most profitable and the most differentiating in the marketplace. If you want to win the better work, you need the entire team using the same growth playbook.

Think of it this way. IT uses agile practices. Accounting operates on agreed-upon principles. Manufacturing has Six Sigma. Why the heck wouldn't your growth use a playbook that scales?

Every other important business process has a common system. Growth should too.

A common playbook helps everyone accomplish more, faster.

My low point created a high point. That pressure I felt long ago pushed me to create a system that worked for me. Then I shared it and evolved it over decades to create something that will work for you and your entire team.

We've created a team implementation guide for *Give to Grow* to help you scale the learnings across a team. Go to givetogrow.info to get it.

And now, having helped tens of thousands of professionals, I want to widen the aperture and help even more people. I've always looked up to the Warren Buffetts and Betty Whites of the world who keep working into their nineties because they love their work so much. I'm devoted to this topic so deeply I hope to keep helping until I can't help anymore. I did the work so you won't have to.

Give to Grow will show you how to develop relationships where everyone wins, including you. Your clients will win because together you'll drive positive change. Your teams will win because they'll be busy doing the work they were meant to do. And you'll win because you'll be in control of your career, doing the work you want for the clients you want.

And when you do that, you'll make the impact you want.

Everyone winning is always the winning move.

Chapter 3

Doing the Work and Winning the Work

Here's one of the biggest insights I've ever had:

Doing the Work ≠ Winning the Work

One more time: not a little different, *completely* different. They're exact opposites.

The top reason most professionals fail at learning how to Win the Work is that they keep making the same moves they did Doing the Work and expecting the same outcomes. And that doesn't end well. →

Some simple examples are as follows:

- In Doing the Work, you have to manage what's in and out of scope, making sure not to give too much away. Optimize profitability, utilization, and realization.

  But in Winning the Work, you want to give people things. Optimize helpfulness, proactiveness, and generosity.

- In Doing the Work, you should expect a 100 percent response rate from your clients, letting the client be your positive behavioral reinforcement. You win when you get a response.

  But in Winning the Work, you should expect a very low response rate, so you have to build your own systems for positive reinforcement. You win when you hit Send.

- In Doing the Work, you want to share great answers with the client. The client says, "Great meeting, we got a lot done."

  But in Winning the Work, you want to ask great questions. The client says, "Great meeting, you understand me and my situation and guided me to the simple next step."

There are so many more. The list goes on and on. Here's a table to get your mind around the two mindsets. Night and day. Black and white. Doing and Winning! ➜

	Doing the Work	Winning the Work
Clients respond	always	rarely
Emails are	long and offer clarity	short and offer help
Communication is	predictable and comfortable	fluid and uncomfortable
You win with	the best answers	the best questions
It's best to go in with	a full presentation	a blank page

	Doing the Work	Winning the Work
You give away	very little and manage to scope	as much as needed to create demand
Feedback is	quick and consistent	slow and irregular
Effort is rewarded	immediately	in the future

Doing the Work creates certainty for others. **Winning the Work creates possibility for others.**

Aren't the differences in that table crazy? Every strategy, tactic, move, and method that works for Doing the Work doesn't work for Winning the Work. You need a different mindset for each and the ability to quickly toggle between them.

All the actions you take in Doing the Work serve others by creating *certainty* by using your expertise to take a predefined outcome and get it done right, on time, and within budget.

All the actions you take in Winning the Work serve others by creating *possibility* by using your expertise to explore all the possible outcomes, decide what should be done, and then guide them toward the best approach to take, including choosing you.

These are completely different mindsets and moves.

Here's what happens if you use your Doing the Work skills to Win the Work: it won't work.

You won't get results. And when you don't get results, you'll do less or just quit. This is why so many people don't make the transformation. They apply their old thinking to the new role. They use the Doing the Work moves in Winning the Work situations. They don't work. And then they quit.

I'll show you how to Win the Work in a way that works. You'll focus on helping over anything else. Long term over short term, relationships over invoices. Give to Grow.

Remember that quote at the beginning of the book? I wake up every morning looking to help my friends succeed, and some of them just happen to be clients. That's the mindset you want. You're going to help your current and future friends succeed. Some will end up being clients and some won't, but overall, you'll win far more work than others and do it in ways that help everyone win. You'll help every day in specific strategic ways that'll have the highest chance of success. And when you do that, it feels authentic and great. And commercial results follow.

Here's what to remember from this short chapter:

Get great at both Winning the Work and Doing the Work mindsets, including how to quickly toggle between them.

The skills are different, so you'll want to learn both. And you'll want to master the ability to know which one is needed at a given time and quickly switch modes between them. The rest of the book will dive into the details of how to do this, but for now, here's your first Pro Tip of many I'll share.

Pro Tip: Because the mindsets and moves are completely different, it can help to batch your Doing the Work and Winning the Work into separate, larger time blocks when possible. The transition between the two mindsets creates friction, so you'll reduce that friction with fewer transitions. Block off time early in the day for Winning the Work activities when you're fresh and it will feel great to knock them out. You won't always be able to do this, but it can be a game changer, especially for the proactive time you want to invest in deepening relationships.

Let's close out Chapter 3. Keep your focus and actions on the long-term relationship. Those actions will stack up over time, creating an unstoppable relationship advantage.

Yes, there's a lot more to it than that—I'll show you every move you need to memorize. Like learning who to help. And how much. And how to offer your help. I'll break it down into simple steps. I'll show you the science. That's what this book is about: the mindset and the moves. You'll get it all.

Next stop: relationship success.

Chapter 4

Relationship Success Isn't Random

Here are the most common questions I get about relationships:

- Who should I invest in?
- How much and how often?
- When do I know to speed up or slow down?

The answers are in the research, and the best researcher on relationships is Adam Grant.[1]

"You *have* to read this!" That's what countless people told me when Adam's book *Give and Take* came out. And these weren't random people—they were those I respected the most. The universe was shouting at me. *Pay attention to this!*

---

1 To save precious book space and add the most value to you, I won't note the rest of the academic citations, but if you want all of them (and there are a lot), just download them at givetogrow.info.

You might be familiar with the book's research. Adam identified three types of people:

- Takers who are selfish, trying to take as much as possible
- Matchers who try to be fair, negotiating an equal trade in each exchange
- Givers who act generously, trying to give every chance they can

The book shows who's the most successful, but come on, I *knew* the answer before I even cracked it open. Givers, of course! I was so sure of myself I demoted the book in my queue for months, thinking, *Why read a book that won't give me an insight?* When I finally started it, my eyes widened and my head tilted back as I realized how wrong I was. The insights were so profound they unlocked something in me.

Unlike the Matchers and Takers, who formed single clusters with similar outcomes, the Givers split into two groups—some were by far the most successful, but the rest were the least successful.

What gives with Givers? Why were some super successful and some flailing failures who burned out? The successful Givers were *strategic* about their giving, which Adam calls being Otherish, or what I like to call Strategic Givers.

Here's what you need to know from *Give and Take*, blending Adam's insights with my own experience:

- Strategic Givers focus their giving on the most important relationships that can meaningfully help *them*, like internal champions or external partners that can choose, influence, and refer. *Focus your investments toward higher potential payoffs.*
- At the same time, Strategic Givers give without expecting *anything* in return. *Give without keeping score.*
- Strategic Givers help others as much as possible but box in their time to create boundaries. Limit your giving based on your availability so you can avoid burnout and getting burned. *Know how to say no.*

Strategic Givers help others and do so in a way that helps themselves.

Guess what falls out of that insight? Process.

There's a Process to Give to Grow, and It's Not Random

You want to help others and make an impact. So if helping is the obvious move, why does it seem like there's randomness in relationships? Why do some professionals seem to get lucky and others don't?

Strategic Givers are, guess what, strategic about their giving. Being a Strategic Giver means being willing to give more than you receive but still keeping your own interests in sight.

When you focus on relationships, growth isn't random—it's reliable.

Here's the equation. There are two sides to giving: someone helping and someone receiving help. We control the helping side, so that isn't random at all. We can choose who we help, how much, and when. We can think in terms of bets and be strategic in these decisions.

So the only real randomness is in the uncontrollable parts: where influential people are at the moment (organization and level), how much they can buy (buying authority and current budget), and what problems they have. These variables seem big, but they're small compared to what we can control.

The successful professional invests in others' success, both strategically and consistently, gaining personal leverage over time. I've seen young relationship-focused consultants go through our programs and become the youngest partner their firm has ever elected. And I've seen older experts come out of their industry laterally and develop bulky books of business in record time.

Strategic Givers win more, win more often, and win bigger engagements.

Young or old, just starting or tenured, they consistently, proactively, and strategically invest in relationships, which creates their own luck and amplifies their impact.

I use these practices myself, investing to build relationships and systems to increase my leverage each day. I'll invest about a thousand hours in writing and bringing this book to market, which will give me the ability to hand it to someone in ten seconds, giving them insights they can use forever.

I've invested over twenty years perfecting and certifying others to teach our comprehensive GrowBIG training system, which gives me the ability to invite a prospect or friend to a public class, completely changing their career trajectory in a five-minute conversation.

And just recently, I invested the time and money to have over forty authors and influencers come to my home for a two-day mastermind so we could all meet and help each other. I have no idea what will come of it, but it was worth every second and penny. It was magic!

All of these investments followed the three elements I gathered from Adam Grant and our own growth.

The best invest in what and who has the highest payoff, do so with no expectation of any specific return, and say no to everything else.

I enjoy thinking through the math of it. For example, I expect my investment in this book to create demand for tens of thousands of new trainees, even though I don't know who exactly that'll be. I expect the thousands of hours I've spent perfecting our GrowBIG training system to pay off because every person we impact will tell their friends and colleagues about the experience, saying, "You *have* to go through this training!" And even though the Mastermind I mentioned cost as much as a wedding, I expect the investment of time and money will pay off 10x or more, even though I don't have any specific expectations for any particular person that attended. The experience changed forty people's lives, including mine, and that'll come back around in unexpected and exciting ways. The potentiality of high-leverage investments excites me. That's where the fun is.

At this point, I feel like I'm running a marathon with tens of thousands of clients, colleagues, and friends cheering me on as I go, with many even running alongside me for parts of the race. Every step forward is more progress: progress with those we've helped and progress in the leverage I have to help even more. It's about positively impacting the most people possible.

That's the race I want to run. And we're all making a meaningful impact together.

This line from Adam's tenth-anniversary reflection of *Give and Take* summed everything up for me:

"I didn't have to convince people that helping others is the best way to succeed. Helping others is the most *meaningful* way to succeed."

Give to Grow Is More than a Title

Give to Grow is a mindset.

Give to Grow means strategically and consistently *giving* so you can exponentially grow your impact over time.

Giving has a broad definition. It means proactively staying in touch, helping your clients even when they can't buy from you, and doing this consistently so that you're at the top of their minds when a need arises. Giving means the client has an enjoyable experience in every interaction, so they're always a little better off after talking to you. And giving means sharing your expertise in ways that result in deeper relationships and more frequent and larger purchases of your services.

Escalating your giving over time in the areas with the highest expected payoff is the winning strategy.

Growing has a broader definition too. Of course, growing means growing your business. But it also means growing the number of your relationships with clients, colleagues, and other partners. Growing means deepening the relationship with each person. And growing means building your *own* development skills so that every hour you spend on development work is more and more efficient over time. Growing means growing your ability to grow your impact even more as time goes on.

There are two reasons to focus on giving and growing. First, winning more and higher-order work will be the best correlation to your future success. Those who bring in the work have more control and impact. Second, the world will naturally *help* you improve your Doing the Work, but the world will *distract* you from improving your Winning the Work.

You have to intentionally focus on getting great at giving and growing.

When you do, you'll not only win more directly but also start making your own luck. You'll create a corps of supporters cheering you on and helping you succeed. Things will get easier over time as you deepen more relationships and get more efficient with each move you make. And you'll feel good because everyone will be winning when they're around you. Maybe it's anti-sales; maybe it's pro-relationship. Either way, it's important, and we can summarize it in this sentence:

A great deal might make your year, but a great relationship can make your career.

That's why Give to Grow is a mindset.

They win.

You win.

Everyone wins!

Chapter 5

Your New Level of Performance

So, what outcomes should we expect?

We now know that the Winning the Work moves are the opposite of what works when Doing the Work. And we also know that giving is the key to growing. But some people think all this giving stuff is woo-woo and won't work.

They're wrong. Here's the data.

The Greats Take Things to Another Level

I stumbled into some startling statistics while writing this book.

I had several clients over a short period of time mention they had a team member whose financial results were far above their norm. *Don't tell anyone, but she's got a $___ million book of business. Insane!* After hearing a similar secret from four clients in five days, I wondered...how many more are like this? The universe was begging me to explore.

After calling and texting several clients, the results started coming in, and they surprised even me, a former actuary who loves guessing games where the answer is a number. I imagined myself as Bob Barker on *The Price Is Right*, finding the astonishing answer to a simple question: What's the difference between your average performer and your Top Performer's annual production?

The results? Almost everyone I surveyed answered within a certain range, and all the numbers were big: 10x to 25x! The most common answer (possibly because this was informal research and people were rounding their numbers) was 10x. So for example, if an organization's average annual book of business for an individual was $5 million, they had one person whose book was between $50 million and $125 million.

Maybe more importantly, *every* organization I contacted had a massive multiple, meaning the difference between average and top performance at every organization I talked to was between 8x and 30x. Let that sink in. For books of business, having a normal distribution is abnormal. And keep in mind, this multiple isn't over the lowest performer, it's over the *average*. That blows me away. I've since asked leaders in industries and functions that can't as easily measure financial results, and they say these rough multiples are true in their spaces too.

The broader research backs up the idea that Top Performers generate multiples in value versus the average. John E. Hunter and his research team found that positions with higher job complexity correlated to higher variance and higher multiples. Guess what role they found to be the highest? Roles that involved "selling," which had over twice the variance in outcomes of even the most complex non-sales roles. Yes, roles involving business development work have a *much* higher variability in performance than any other role they reviewed. McKinsey similarly found that "very high complexity" roles had 9x the difference between Top Performers and average performers. I'll bet if you start looking you'll see similar results in your organization, too.

It's worth saying again:

Top Performers typically achieve 10x or more than the average performer.

Let's dig deeper. Many people think the Top Performers "were born with it." Not true. I know them. I've trained them. Some are my best friends. I get to see inside their lives, learning how they think and how they approach their craft.

Top Performers look at growth differently. They worry about staying in touch with their current relationships whether there's something for them to buy right now or not. They worry about creating demand for work three years out.

The biggest difference I see between Top Performers and everyone else is that they treat growth strategies and actions as their highest priority.

Annual growth themes. Weekly priorities. Daily actions. Over and over.

Most professionals fit relationship development in when they can, maybe in that open slot at 4:30 p.m., most times kicking it to the next day. Top Performers Win the Work first and Do the Work second. First in the morning, first in the week. If they have a late night, they're finishing Doing the Work, not Winning it. Most professionals often get "too busy," letting relationship development blow in the winds of Doing the Work, but Top Performers are consistent. They reach out when they're busy and even more when they're (seldomly) slower.

How Top Performers approach learning is also different. Most professionals treat it randomly. Random hallway conversations. Random internal email chains. Random "What are you doing?" conversations at the big annual meeting.

Top Performers make learning the craft of relationship development the most important part of relationship development. Dog-eared books and memorized frame-works. Folders and databases of assets and approaches. Reflections on what went well and what didn't in the meeting last Tuesday, bathing in the regret of the smallest mistake. And they use all of these tools to learn and to improve.

And you know what? This 10x Top Performer insight is the best news of all.

It means you can learn this stuff. It means you can help others in ways that also help you. And it means you can have an impact that's bigger than you ever thought possible.

There's a system for growth, just like there's a system for delivery.

It's learnable. It's predictable. And it's scalable.

And while most Top Performers had to figure it out on their own, you're holding it in your hands right now.

Here's how Give to Grow will teach you to be a Top Performer.

First, Lose the Lies

Let's face the facts. There are a lot of headwinds on this journey.

There is so much misinformation coming from others, including downright lies that are shared like they're universal truths:

- "You're born with it or you're not."
- "Just take clients to great dinners."
- "No one can do it like Russ can."

None of these are true. *At all*. I'll share the science that backs me up, but for now, have hope.

And even if you lose the lies others share with you, you have to worry about your own. The worst lies are the ones we tell ourselves. I'm too busy. I didn't join this profession to sell. I don't want to be a nag.

The lies we tell ourselves are the worst, because there's no one else to tell us they're false.

In Section Two, I'll show you the top five lies we've found people tell themselves, along with how to spot and replace each of them with the truth.

Next, Use Your Gifts

Here's the good news...and the truth:

- Client retention and growth is a learnable skill.
- It's not rocket science; it's brain science.
- It's learnable, practical, and repeatable.
- And the biggest beauty in this book? It's focused on *relationships*.

In Section Three, I'll show you how you can invest in long-term relationships with four gifts you can always rely on. This will let you win the work you want in a way your clients will love. Doesn't that sound fun? You can reach your goals by helping others reach theirs. You'll give. You'll grow. Give to Grow.

Finish with Flawless Implementation

Learning the lies and leveraging the gifts is one thing, but you need to *implement* them. Section Four will teach you how to build systems to have success in the short term and in the long term. All of this will teach you how to win more of the work you want with the clients you want. And you know what?

Winning is fun.

Chapter 6

Do This Now

1. **Think of someone you've been meaning to reach out to.**
2. **Open a new email.**
3. **Type your version of the following:**

Hi Jonathan,

It's been a long time! Would love to hear what's going on in your world. Maybe I can find some ways to be helpful. Are you free Thursday at 2 p.m. ET?
—Mo

P.S. Can't wait to share what's going on with the family.

4. Press Send.
5. Don't overthink it.
6. Press Send.

Let's debrief. *Didn't it feel good?*

This activity gets you going. Small, consistent actions like this create a relationship advantage because you'll have more meaningful Give to Grow conversations. Ask to catch up. Look to give first. Invest in their success with no expectation of anything in return. *Be Otherish.*

It's powerful. It'll help you. *And when you talk, find a way to help them.*

Section Two:
The Lies

The worst lies are the lies you tell yourself.

I could never do it like Mike does, so why try? Diane didn't respond to my last email, so she doesn't need my help. I'm not sure what they need. I'm not sure what to do. They're really busy. I'm too busy to reach out. Lie. Lie. Lie.

The lies you create are powerful because there's no one to tell you they're wrong. You invent a story and believe it. Process complete. Barrier erected. Progress halted.

You'll feel some often while others pop up randomly, jack-in-the-box style. Some will slow you down a bit, and others will Muhammad Ali you to the mat. You'll tell yourself a million lies over your career, but they will always fall into five concrete categories, and once you know those, you're set to spot them. And once spotted, you can solve them.

This section will show you the lies to lose and the solutions to use. Most people think their biggest worry should be their competition and what they're doing. It's not.

Your biggest worry should be *you* and what *you're* doing—or not doing.

It's time to make your five invisible barriers visible, then remove them one by one. Here's the first of the five.

Chapter 7

I Can't Do That

Let's start with the biggest lie of them all: I can't do that.

Some people see this lie like a freight train coming down the tracks, telling them they aren't good at any growth skills. I didn't become a _____ to sell.

That version is easy to spot because it's so loud. But for others, this lie is much sneakier and harder to see, creeping in as a tiny thought, then silently spreading, growing stronger and stronger.

Here are some other specific examples we often hear in our training sessions: →

I hate the idea of selling.

I just like doing the work.

I'm not good at reaching out.

I'm not good at going to dinner.

I'm an introvert—I'm not good at networking.

I'm only good with people I've known for a long time.

I'm not good at chit chat.

I can't build a book of business like Debbie did.

The Lies

Those are more common than most would expect, so if you're feeling one of those, you're not alone. Those are the big ones and easier to spot.

Here are the sneakier versions, which isolate one skill and say things like "I'm not good at ____." We've seen people fill in that blank with everything imaginable.

I'm not good at...

- Bringing in bigger deals
- Talking to the C-suite
- Talking about our _____ offering
- Talking about our pricing
- Cross-selling
- Differentiating us versus our biggest competitor

Pick your poison. Choose your own misadventure. Whatever doesn't work for you. Seriously, these more nuanced examples can get to anyone. And once this lie is in, it can win. You have to notice it and eradicate it right away.

Here's a story that can bring this one to life. Along with our group- and organization-wide training, we do a lot of one-on-one coaching. The personal coaching lets us dive deeper and in more specific ways. In one case, a senior consultant was already having tremendous success relative to his peers, but inside, he didn't feel confident. In his words, "It feels like I have a bunch of random acts of lunch, and it seems to work, but I can't seem to stay consistent or avoid getting busy."

We'd seen this movie before! So, we staffed him with a top coach and got to work. The beauty of one-on-one coaching is you can personalize the approach. Our coach dug into all his systems: habits, tech, task management, and more. After just five sessions, our coach messaged me, "Mo, Ivan told me our coaching has advanced his skills by years! I'm having so much fun seeing him succeed."

Another coaching client was in the top 10 percent of originations in his law firm—already viewed as a Top Performer—but confided in us that he didn't think he was good at creating and fostering new relationships. So, you guessed it, we shared our system of sixteen different ways to generate leads and coached him around the three he was most excited about.[2] He quickly dialed in each new skill to take his career to the next level.

In both cases, each professional went from "I can't" to "I can" once they had an approach to absorb. Half their battle was knowing these skills are learnable, and the other half was being given a proven system to learn. You can go from "I can't" to "I can" too, no matter what your "I can't" is.

---

2 You can download the list of lead generation methods at givetogrow.info.

Now that we've got this lie tackled and tied, here's how you can overcome it.

The Truth

Carol Dweck is a rock star researcher and professor at Stanford. Her work shows that the view you adopt of yourself affects the way you live your life, the results you'll get, and the impact you'll have.

She's found that you can have one of two mindsets for any perspective. A fixed mindset implies your abilities are carved in stone, that they can't and won't change. A growth mindset implies you can get better—even if it's a small amount—if you focus on improving. My favorite quote of hers is: "The fixed mindset makes you concerned with how you'll be judged; the growth mindset makes you concerned with improving." We've struck a vein of mindset gold!

It gets better. She's got a simple hack we can use to take the power back from the lie "I can't."

If you ever hear yourself thinking, "I'm not good at _____," do one thing. Add a *yet* to the end of your sentence. "I'm not good at _____ *yet*."

This one simple change acknowledges your fears and unlocks your potential. It's time for a short and sharp activity to guide your positive progress.

I'm not good at...

yet.

Now, let's build on Carol's mental moves. Upon his passing, researcher K. Anders Ericsson was viewed as the #1 expert in the world on (get this) expertise. He's the 10,000 hours guy and easily the worldwide expert on expertise. What a cool gig!

He found, irrefutably, that any complex skill is both learned and earned. Sure, one Top Performer might have been born with the gift of gab and another with powerful persistence. But growth skills are a roll up of hundreds of smaller skills. And *no one* was born with more than a few.

We see this in our work in training and coaching tens of thousands of professionals. Show me a Top Performer and I'll show you someone that worked at it, someone that sweated every detail, improving in small ways over years and years.

Others don't witness the work Top Performers put in over years and decades to become great, so they incorrectly assume they were born with it.

Here's the thing: you'll hear about it if you ask them. Ask them how hard they've worked. Ask them about how they keep in touch with people even when they're busy. Ask them how to approach the craft of relationship development.

Asking specific questions like this will give you specific answers. You'll see the Top Performer is made, not born. Every time. Some people say practice makes perfect. That's a high bar. We look at it differently. Practice makes progress. Ericsson said it best: "Consistently and overwhelmingly, the evidence showed that experts are always made, not born."

I mentioned Ericsson led the science behind the ten-thousand-hour rule. The problem is that others bastardized the idea, and what's commonly discussed isn't what he actually said. The misconception is that he meant that ten thousand hours of work will *always* lead to expertise—just put the time in and you'll be in great shape. But in truth, he was very clear that raw hours don't always correlate with improvement.[3] Quantity of practice is important, but his research showed the quality is important too.

He found what sets what we call Top Performers apart from others is the quantity and quality of their mental representations. These allow them to react quickly and effectively because they've memorized their moves and rehearsed their responses. Think of how fast an athlete reacts to a given situation. Their response is reflexive, automatic, fluid. Smooth. They do drills

3 Check out his book *Peak* for more on this. Or, if you want something faster, go to givetogrow.info for a link to an entertaining and insightful fifty-minute *Freakonomics Radio* interview with Ericsson. Highly recommend!

over and over until an important move is second nature. Top Performers in our world do the same thing, making hard things look easy. You can do it too.

Practice doesn't make perfection. Practice makes progress.

He called the system elite performers use to improve "deliberate practice." It has a long scientific definition, but for our purposes it comes down to these three killer concepts:

- Be intentional about what skill you'll work on next.
- Take risks by stretching just outside your comfort zone and practicing one precise skill.
- Get fast feedback from people around you so you can figure out what to change and what to keep. This works best with an experienced coach watching and giving you immediate feedback, but if that's not possible, ask others who can watch you perform.

Here's an activity to feel the power of deliberate practice.

I am good at...

right now.

Wasn't that fun? You've learned a lot over the years. You've built deep expertise. *You've learned*. And you can use the same methods to improve your Winning the Work skills. No matter where you're at in your proficiency, deliberate practice will power you to a new level.

Now pick one of the skills you wrote down, maybe one you're quite proud of learning, and reflect back on the time periods where you made the most progress.

You likely had a coach, a guide, or someone who was ahead of you and could give you quick feedback. That was deliberate practice. Now, let's summarize the solution— what we can do to add even more skills with speed.

The Solution

So, here's your summary of our first lie, along with your solution looking forward:

1. Learn to see the lie "I can't." If you see it, you can solve it.
2. Reframe your brain to say, "I can't ____ *yet.*"
3. Make a plan to improve. Get an expert to guide you if it's important.

It's that simple. If you're in the 10th percentile, you can sprint to 60th, above average. In our trainings, we've seen people just starting out improve that much in a matter of months.

If you're in the 90th percentile and already known as a Top Performer, you can make minor changes that have massive impact. Just going from the 90th to 95th percentile could mean a 2x to 3x impact in your outcomes. That's meaningful!

No matter where you're at, small, consistent improvements lead to big results. Set up your own annuity of awesomeness.

OK, great news. You've lassoed the first lie. But there are still four more to wrangle.

Chapter 8

I Don't Know What to Do

Great news! You've bulldozed the lie "I can't do that." That's important, because if you think "I can't do that," you won't.

Here's the next lie to lose: I'm not sure what to do. "I can't" stops you from starting. "I'm not sure what to do" sways you to delay.

Delay is a devilish device. You think you're making progress, deciding to do something later. But "I'm not sure what to do" knows that later rarely comes. Here are some of the versions of this lie we commonly hear: →

I don't have anything meaningful or new to share.

I don't have an excuse to reach out.

I need to wait till ___ happens.

I'm not sure what they need.

I might be bothering them.

I don't know what their priorities are.

It's been forever since we caught up so it's awkward.

Someone else has a better relationship with them.

That's a lot of lies. It's amazing how creative we can be to avoid acting! But, nice news, we're going to remove this lie like the rest. Here's how.

All these specific lies boil down to three sub-lies:

- I don't know what they want.
- I don't like what we have.
- I only interact with them in certain ways or times.

Here's the simple solution to the lie "I don't know what to do," no matter how it presents itself:

It's always your move, and there's always a way to be helpful.

A story brings this to life. See if you see yourself in it. Years ago, we were leading our first training cohort in one of the top professional service firms in the world. These were super-smart, highly technical experts striving to make a positive impact. We were on the second day of GrowBIG training and talking about outreach when one of the senior consultants abruptly looked up at the ceiling. You could almost see the thought bubble over his right shoulder.

So I asked, "Hey Matt, I'm curious, what are you thinking?" He said:

I just had a major unlock. I've been thinking about client interactions like I'm playing tennis. I only volley back to them only after they volley back to me. I'm always waiting for them to respond before I respond.

He continued, with an insightful gem:

I now realize I need to think of client outreach like I'm practicing my serve with a tennis pro, not volleying back and forth. I just have to keep serving up value, regardless of if they hit a particular ball back to me or not.

Yes! We all feel the lie "I'm not sure what to do" from time to time. This sweet talker will sneak into your mind at your lowest points, like when you're worried or insecure. And once it's in, it'll take over. Here's how to handle it.

The Truth

Memorize this mantra: It's always your move. Almost all professionals overthink timing, so I'm emphasizing action to get past it. Remembering that "it's always your move" will get you to act.

We'll use "it's always your move" to handle each of the three sub-lies, and here's the first: I don't know what they want. Get ready—this solution is mind-blowing. You might need extra sleep tonight.

If you don't know what the client wants, ask them.

There are so many ways to do this, but it's usually best in an in-person or live virtual interaction, not over email. Here's a way you can ask for the live meeting:

> Josh,
>
> It's been forever.
>
> One thing my best clients do is share their broader priorities with me on an ongoing basis, like quarterly. If you'll invest that time with me, I can look for ways we can invest in your success. How's lunch sound to start?
>
> Mo
>
> P.S. Can't wait to hear about your trip to Breckenridge!

Or, you can weave it into a meeting you've already got:

> Shawn, before we jump in, I've got an idea.
> I meet with my best clients periodically, usually
> quarterly, to check in. For us, I envision I can
> learn your priorities and then look for ways to
> be helpful. No charge for this—it's a win-win.
> What do you think of us setting a quarterly
> catch-up meeting like that?

Bonus! You get *three* Pro Tips this time.

Pro Tip 1: Notice the black-belt ninja move in those suggestions, asking for a *series* of catch-up meetings instead of just one. This is an annuity of helpfulness! Use this over and over for the rest of your career.

Pro Tip 2: Also notice how short the email is. One email screen on a phone is about fifty words, so stay in that range. You'll get faster replies more often when you limit your development emails to a nifty fifty.

Pro Tip 3: Everyone reads a P.S. Use that precious real estate to make a connection.

OK, now let's tackle the second sub-lie of the three: I don't like what we have. This sub-lie surfaces around specific desires: for instance, wanting a better document with updated qualifications or content.

We can get pretty creative thinking of ways to delay, but here's the thing: the client doesn't expect what you expect they expect. The client wants you to use your broad expertise to solve their specific problems. Said bluntly:

The client doesn't want your documents, they want a helpful conversation.

Put yourself in their shoes. Do you think they're waking up in the morning wishing someone would walk them through a slightly updated case study? That they're sipping a cappuccino dreaming someone will walk them through their offerings in a PowerPoint, complete with a slide showing their best client logos? No, they're not. They don't want the version you have now, and they don't want the 2.4 percent-better version you have in your mind.

The client wants helpful conversation. Let me be bold. You're ready to have a helpful conversation if they called you *right now*. Sure, you'd like a little more time to prepare, but any potential client could learn from you in this exact second.

Let me dial up the boldness to eleven, because that's one better than ten. They have something they're struggling with that you and your organization can help them with right now, and every week you spend delaying, wishing you had a 2.4 percent-better *something* on your side, is another week you're not helping them.

Your solution, again, is that it's always your move. Offer a helpful conversation with the best expert you can find. I know. Crazy, huh? Getting past your own self is the barrier. This one's so simple I won't offer any scripts. Just do it. Make the offer. Put the book down and do it right now. Act.

Here's the version of "it's always your move" to tackle if you ever feel that second of the three sub-lies, "I don't like what we have." I'll build on what we already covered.

The client wants a helpful conversation, and it's your responsibility to offer it to them.

So offer it to them. Case closed. Barrier blasted.

Here's the last sub-lie: I only interact with them in certain ways or times. Remember all of our previous specific examples. This "certain ways and times" lie can surface in two major ways, timing or topical:

- Timing, like only reaching out at a certain time of year or when specific things are about to happen, such as a client conference, economic cycle, or time of year.
- Topical, like only talking about professional things. Or only talking about personal things. Or any other kind of "we've only ever talked about _____" things.

There's lots to unpack! Whatever your version of the above is, remember a line my friend Tim Grahl blurted out to me when I was telling myself a tall tale: "That's quite a story you're telling yourself!"

Think of your longest-standing, deepest relationships. Maybe it's your best friend from back in the day. Or that favorite nephew. Or a client who's also a great friend. Your best relationships started with one topic and evolved to explore many more over time. However things started, they didn't end there. And however things have been with a client doesn't have to be how they'll always be.

The best relationships evolve. They grow, broaden, and deepen. Yet again, here's another application of "it's always your move."

It's always your move to broaden and deepen the relationship.

My friend Michael Melcher wrote about this in his excellent book *Your Invisible Network*.[4] He defines a "bid" as taking a 15 percent risk in a relationship, doing something a touch beyond what's been done before, something that's not a big risk but could create a small advancement or broadening.

---

4 Michael dropped a ton of insights in an interview we had on my podcast, *Real Relationships, Real Revenue*. Check out the link at givetogrow.info.

Here are some 15 percent bid questions from our comprehensive GrowBIG training:

- I'd enjoy going to dinner to get to know each other better. What do you think?
- What's next for you?
- Where would you like your career to go in the future?
- How's your year going? What would make a strong finish?
- What are you focused on in the upcoming year?
- What kinds of things do you do outside of work?
- What are you looking forward to right now?
- What kinds of people would you like to be introduced to?
- If you could wave a magic wand and improve your function in a certain way, what would it be?

And here are some questions about you and your organization:

- How do you think our organization can better differentiate itself?
- How can we do a better job of serving your organization?
- What can we focus on to make you look great in the future?
- What one thing should we make sure we do to help us all succeed in the next phase of our work?
- Who else would benefit from knowing us in your organization?

Some of these can seem a little scary, especially for certain clients. Ask the easier versions first, ones that are just 15 percent bids based on what you've discussed before. You won't get a yes every time, but remember this: the more you ask, the more you'll receive.

It'll probably be higher than this, but let's just say you get a positive response to a 15 percent bid 60 percent of the time. The professional that asks to evolve a relationship 10x over another is going to get 10x more yeses. If an average performer makes ten bids a year, they'll get six, but a Top Performer that makes a hundred will get sixty. 10x!

To get great at growth, you have to get out of the perfectionist Doing the Work mindset and get into the Winning the Work mindset.

Don't expect 100 percent success. A 60 percent success rate in evolving the relationship means you won't advance 40 percent of the time. Don't see these as failures; see them as *not yets*. Keep asking. It's always your move.

The Solution

Here are some practical tips to make positive progress. From now on, weave this question into every relevant meeting you have, whether it's a first-time introduction, a check-in conversation, or a delivery meeting:

> Hey Francesca, I get a lot of interesting things across my desk in my role as a senior leader at _____. **What kinds of things are interesting to you right now?** If I know your priorities, I can shoot over thought pieces, invite you to events, introduce you to great people, and do lots of other things that might be helpful to you.

Once they start talking, ask follow-up questions. Dig in deep. And once you have topics chosen, ask them how they like to receive information. Do they like email or a certain messaging app? A phone call? Quarterly or monthly in-person meetings?

Weaving this into meetings is gold for three reasons: it shows you're focused on the relationship, they'll be opting into your future outreaches because they're telling you what they like, and you'll broaden the relationship in more ways than you can expect.

If you want to invest in someone but haven't been able to have that conversation yet, you can still act. It's always your move. Just make a 15 percent bid. Make an offer to have a helpful conversation on a topic they might like. Invite them to an event. Send an article. If they respond positively, great! You've expanded your relationship. If they decline or don't respond, great! That's information on what they aren't interested in. (And maybe a prompt to ask what they are.)

Let's go into full actuarial mode, leveraging the power of compounding. Fifteen percent growth doesn't seem like much, but it's a ton, doubling with compounding in about five quick cycles. So if you grow by 15 percent in each interaction over five meeting cycles, you've doubled the depth of your relationship. That's way more than most expect. Just keep advancing.

I need to connect with...

So let's close out this chapter, replacing "I'm not sure what to do" with "I know several things I can do." Remember this alongside "it's always your move."

Disconnect yourself from the outcome and focus on what's in your control.

Don't invent and worry about possible outcomes. That'll cause you to pause. Don't think in terms of Doing the Work, where every outreach will get a response. Instead, just keep offering helpfulness. Keep adding value. Your win isn't when they answer; your win is when you offer value.

If it's in person...

You win when you make the offer.

And if it's a written offer...

You win when you hit Send.

Disconnect yourself from the outcome. Offer more value more often to get more responses. It's always your move.

Keep practicing that serve!

Chapter 9

I Might Do It Wrong

Whew! We bowled over another barrier. So, what's the next nuisance to nix?

This next lie is a skulker and a schemer: I might do it wrong.

Notice the lies are layered. You have to get through the first two to get to this one. You've got the client in mind. You know you can make the move, and you know it's your move to make. The fear here is that you'll do it wrong. Here's what we hear people say: →

I don't want
to ask dumb
questions.

I don't know the
content well enough
to talk about it.

I'm out of touch
with the rest
of our team
and might say
something
wrong.

I'm afraid
I don't know
the answers
to questions
they might ask.

I'm not important enough
to meet with them.

We don't have
a brand name,
so we might
shoot ourselves
in the foot.

The Lies

This lie's roots come from perfectionism and being too self-reliant. You're used to being perfect. Perfect project execution. Perfect meetings. Perfect lists and emails. Never missing a thing, always gaining ground. Always perfect.

"What got you here won't get you there" is especially profound with this lie, this fear of doing something wrong. You're also used to being self-reliant because you are the expert; you're the one everyone else calls for help. This can lead you to always think you're the helper, not someone who needs help.

The Truth

The solution for all the variations of this lie is asking for help. But this is much harder than it appears.

Victor Ottati and his research team validated a mental heuristic they called "earned dogmatism." Their paper states:

> ...social norms dictate that experts are entitled to adopt a relatively dogmatic, closed-minded orientation. As a consequence, situations that engender self-perceptions of high expertise elicit a more closed-minded cognitive style.

They found across six different experiments that the more expert you perceive your abilities to be, the more closed-minded you become! It's ironic that the more we know, the more we have to fight to keep our minds open.

Now, let's add the perspective of Wayne Baker, a professor and researcher who wrote the excellent book *All You Have to Do Is Ask* and a top global expert in why and how to ask for help. He found people have an *extremely* strong reluctance to ask for help; he even calls it a "human dilemma." Here are my favorite among the list of eight forces he's seen that push us away from asking for help:

> We underestimate other people's willingness and ability to help, we overly rely on self-reliance, we perceive there to be a social cost of seeking help, we don't know what to request or how to request it, and we fear seeming selfish.

That's quite a list. His work crystallized for me that we have to worry about not only *barriers* we perceive in asking for help but also strong forces *against* us asking for help. We need help in asking for help!

Here's the scientific good news, which Francis Flynn and Vanessa Lake (now Bohns) found in a study:

People drastically overestimate how many people they need to ask to get help while drastically underestimating how much help they'll get!

Getting past this lie means creating a small, interim step that involves others' help, like a colleague, a client, or a Strategic Partner (someone who has the same or similar clients as you do but who has a noncompetitive and aligned offering). Colleagues are great for getting training on a topic or thinking through how to word something. Clients can be great to bounce ideas off of. And Strategic Partners can add value because they see all sides.

Remember this when asking for help: the deepest relationships are mutually beneficial.

Others *want* to help you. You feel great when you help others, right? Well, others feel great helping you. And you'll bond as you help each other. Great relationships are just friendships with both sides helping each other. And the deepest relationships are the ones where both sides help each other often.

Here are some examples:

- If you're struggling with how to word something with a client or how to bring up a new topic, spend fifteen minutes with a colleague or Strategic Partner. Instant unlock!

- If you're worried you don't know enough about a topic, ask someone to join you that does. Win-win!
- And if you're concerned about how to navigate within a client environment, ask your client for guidance. They'll be glad to help you!

Each of these involves a small, interim step. The closer these get to the client, the more people hesitate. It's easy to think, "I can't ask the client for help!" Yes, you can. Here's how: reframe asking for help as asking for advice. This is great because...

Everyone likes giving advice.

The Solution

So with your new mindset in mind, here are some specific steps you can take.

Talk to someone else. Describe your situation and ask for advice using this template.[5]

Describe something you want, then ask: What would you do if you were me?

---

5   I got this from my friend Marissa King, researcher and author of the book *Social Chemistry*. You guessed it, she was on *Real Relationships, Real Revenue*, and it was a riot! Link at givetogrow.info.

Whether internal or external, this always gets things moving. Within five or ten minutes, there's always a "What if you...?" moment that cuts through the clutter, making the next step clear.

Pro Tip: Having someone like this to interact with often is a game changer. Enter into a little agreement with a Top Performer, peer, boss, Strategic Partner, client, or just someone else that has great ideas. Maybe you even start a small cohort of people learning to be great at growth. Setting up an agreement or group like this will reap the benefits for years to come.

After you unlock a strategic idea, get tactical. Break the big idea into small steps. Maybe you need to find a new expert to bring to the client. Or maybe you need to write a draft email to run past the client relationship leader to get their feedback. Just keep moving.

Asking others for their advice provides a double win because you'll move things forward *and* you'll deepen your relationship.

This is the most difficult for people, but just remember, everyone loves giving advice, and the deepest relationships are mutually beneficial. Everyone likes the feeling of helping others. Your clients are people too. Sure, you can ask too much, but that's rare. Most experts ask far too infrequently.

Hi _____ ,

I am trying to...

What would you do if you were me?

Let's close out this lie by shedding light on the fear of asking for help. You're used to being the expert. You're used to knowing all the answers. That's worked great for you, and it's a strength when you're Doing the Work. But that mindset will limit you when Winning the Work. You already know what to do when Doing the Work, because you've done it before. But when Winning the Work, you're naturally creating something that doesn't yet exist.

Getting others' perspectives will let you see the future missteps you can't currently see. Why walk in a minefield with clown shoes on?

So flip the script. Getting comfortable asking for advice unlocks relationship and business success. It'll deepen your relationships because people see you as human. It'll let you see what to avoid and what to do. It'll enroll others in your success because many times, others will offer to help far beyond what you expect. It even conveys you're a better expert because you're still striving to learn.

Next up is our fourth of the five lies. It impacts more people than any other. I'd love for you to turn the page to see what it is, but I'd like to close this chapter with a clever ending first:

What would you do if you were me?

Chapter 10

I'm Too Busy

Whoa, Nelly, it's the big one!

Everyone feels this lie, from the blue collared to the blue bloods, down the hall and around the world. It transcends level, industry, and age. You've felt it before, and you'll feel it again.

The bad news—this lie is the most likely to harm you. The good news—it's the easiest to spot. Examples include: →

I'm slammed with work now.

I couldn't do anything with them now even if they hired me.

We don't have capacity.

This stuff takes too long, and I don't have time right now.

Those are the no-nuance versions you'll hear in your mind and even say to others. But like the other lies, this trickster can steal your momentum without you seeing it. The stealthier versions sneak in by broadening the lie, postponing your actions with every second- and third-cousin argument related to "I'm too busy":

I've already hit my goals for this year, so why try?

I like the immediate gratification of doing the work and helping the team.

This might not even pay off, so I'm not sure it's worth the effort.

Other people should be doing this.

This is the last thing on my list and never seems to get done.

Honestly, I get distracted with other things that are more enjoyable.

Ever felt any of those? We all have. The first list yells, "I'm so busy, I'm not sure when I'll be able to go to the restroom!" It stops you in your tracks. The second list? It'll sneak up on you without you knowing it, politely nudging you to push off your efforts another day, another week. This lie wins when those days and weeks turn into years:

> Darn! Tiffani got promoted to CEO and I haven't reached out in five years. If I connect now, I'll really look like a self-centered opportunist— best to wait a few more months again.

Either version of this lie results in the same thing: no action and no results.

Let's work on spotting this sucker. Quick exercise: Go back to those two lists and put a star next to any of the versions you've ever felt. Think back on your entire life. How many did you star? Most say it's over half. That's why this lie is so scary. It's the common cold of lies, and everyone can catch it at any time. So let's wash our hands of it once and for all.

The Truth

Here's the mindful mantra for this little liar:

The best time to grow is when you're busiest.

We've largely avoided the word "sell" until now, but if we're using the positive definition of the word, like being proactively helpful, this version is more memorable.

The best time to sell is when you're sold out.

Here's the truth:

Being busy has big benefits.

- When you're busy, you have access to more decision-makers.
- When you're busy, you have the most interesting things to share.
- When you're busy, people value your time.
- When you're busy, you get creative, finding ways to speed things up.
- When you're busy, you've earned the right to be informal and fast.

So, if it's easier to grow when you're busy, why does everyone fall for the "I'm too busy" lie?

They're thinking about growth tasks all wrong, and it grinds growth to a halt. The flawed thinking is that they can only be focused on delivery or development in a given time period. Doing that brings about a mindset of "I don't have time for Winning the Work activities right now." If you've ever thought that, you're sunk before you start.

Here's the truth:

Top Performers integrate delivery *and* development to get the most out of the benefits of being busy.

I want you to delete this phrase from your mind: "I'm either doing development *or* delivery." Your relationship development results are drastically faster when you're busy. You want to capitalize on this.

Here are the top three reasons why Winning the Work is easier when you're busy Doing the Work:

- **Access:** It's easier to get a yes when you have access. One study out of Cornell found a face-to-face ask was 34x more likely to get a yes. Note that's 34 *times* more likely, not 34 percent. In their study, it was the difference between a 2 out of 100 chance of getting a yes over email and a 68 out of 100 chance face to face. 34x! You want to ask while you have access.

- **Insight:** You have the most interesting things to share when you're busy. This goes for the detailed work you're leading with clients and also the thematic trends you can see and share across your work. Your clients want to know what others are doing, what themes you're seeing, and what you're learning—all applied to their unique situation. You want to capitalize on your current knowledge.

- **Value:** Clients can sense when you're busy, so your investments will mean much more to them. There's a mental heuristic bucketed under the word *scarcity* that says, "We humans want more of what there is less of." The less time you have, the more clients will want it. You want to leverage the scarcity of your time because people want you more when you're busy.

Access lets you ask for things with a high chance of a yes. Insight gives you things to share. And value is what the client feels when you're in demand.

This summarizes everything nicely:

The number one thing that signals your expertise is the scarcity of your time, and you should leverage being busy to help, not hurt, your future self.

Pro Tip: You can be both in demand *and* responsive. Consider this a "break glass in case of emergency" Pro

Tip, because you won't use it all the time. But if you're beyond busy, consider telling people directly instead of implying it. For example: "I'm wall-to-wall nonstop for about three weeks, but you're important to me, so I could maybe move an internal meeting Tuesday at 2 p.m. Would that by chance work?" You can shoot yourself in the foot by saying, "It's no big deal" when it really is a big deal. If you're slammed, consider saying it. Your clients will value your efforts more when you do.

Being in demand sends a stronger signal about your worth than your qualifications, representative work, bio, and prestige of who you work for. When you're in demand, the immediate assumption is that you're expensive, your expertise is worth it, and your time is valuable. Scarcity is powerful. Infants as early as age two act on the feeling of scarcity, people buy more when things are scarce, and we think things that are scarce are of higher quality than things that aren't.

The Solution

The best way to see the solution is through a story. Let's say you're working with a prestigious client and the work could grow in many ways. Upside! You're in a meeting with them in the middle of delivery and casually say:

Hey Jeromy, it's been great working with you on this project. I'd really enjoy getting to know more about your goals and find ways to be helpful. Maybe we could have dinner after our project is over in about two months. We can celebrate our work and talk through you and your team's broader mandates. Then I can look for ways to be helpful in the future. I think it would be a lot of fun.

Let's break that down: You have a 34x greater chance of a yes by asking in the meeting than over email in two months. That ask takes about twenty seconds to say, and you'll get a "That sounds great!" response. Maybe the whole discussion will take a minute, including "Sure, contact my assistant and we'll get it on the books now. I'll look forward to that."

Simple, right? The problem is that most people wait till the project is over, thinking they need to bifurcate development from delivery. They're thinking in the "I'm either Doing *or* Winning" mindset. Mistake!

If you wait until the project's over, you'll spend thirty minutes figuring out the perfect email to send Jeromy to ask for dinner, he has a much lower chance of responding (remember, 34x), and there will be a delay if he responds at all. And you waited a few months to make the ask, so it'll take another few months to set up the dinner, if it happens at all.

Let's compare the two approaches. Math alert! Waiting to ask till the project is over means a 90x longer time invested with 1/34th the chance of success, and even *if* the dinner does happen, it's three to six months farther out. More time, less success, and longer time to impact. Waiting = *not* good! Whether you're asking for a dinner to get to know your client, introducing a colleague that might be helpful, or anything else, you don't want to wait.

So right now, do a Find and Replace in your mind. Find every "I'm focused on Doing the Work or Winning the Work" and replace it with "I'm consistently focused on integrating Doing the Work and Winning the Work." That's what Top Performers do, and you should too.

Here's why, loosely applying Newton's laws of motion to relationships. An object at rest stays at rest. An object in motion stays in motion. Going deeper, that object at rest takes a *lot* of force to get it going again, while an object in motion stays in motion with little or no effort at all.

Keeping your relationship development efforts always moving forward is *easy* when you integrate delivery and development. Little efforts keep things moving.

One word summarizes integrating Doing the Work and Winning the Work: priority.

Top Performers prioritize their Winning efforts by consistently doing little things that keep the process moving forward. They integrate their development with their delivery every week. Little efforts done consistently are more effective than much larger efforts done inconsistently.

On the Doing the Work side of things, heroic efforts get the job done. Long weekends and late nights! But you don't want to have that mindset for Winning the Work. Instead, make small strategic investments all the time. Prioritize!

It's easy to spot when someone prioritizes something. They have systems to manage and track themselves. They think about them when planning their week. They do them first thing in the morning before the day blows up. I'll cover a proven process for managing your development work in the last section of this book, but now just reflect on how you prioritize winning your work.

Many professionals fall into the trap of thinking either/ or. I'm doing delivery or development. Doing the Work or Winning the Work. They're missing out on their superpowers of access, insight, and value. No more or. From now on, think *and*.

There aren't many moves you can make in life that take less time to get better results. Integrating development and delivery is one of them. Do that and you'll maintain and even accelerate your momentum. Newton would be proud.

My ONE Thing this week is...

Chapter 11

I'm Going to Look Bad

Time for some fun—we're going to lose the last lie. Be ready, though. This is the Wicked One, the most devilish. It'll prey on your deepest fears, trying to convince you you're not needed, not worthy, and not good enough. Don't let this lie in. And if it sneaks its way in, don't let it win. It's *the fear of looking bad*.

Our workshop surfaces this all the time, and in many ways: →

I don't want to be a pest or nag.

I don't want to come across as salesy.

I can't ask my friends for business.

I'm worried they might not even remember me.

I'm not even sure they need me (or us).

I'm intimidated by them.

The Lies

What help would talking to me be?

They already use someone else.

Someone there doesn't like me (or us).

The person recently canceled on me.

They're already spending a lot with us.

That's our longest lie list yet. This one will attack you in so many ways, preying on your strongest fears in your weakest moments.

We've all felt this one, rarely for some and routinely for others. And as soon as you kick it out, it's working to find a new way in. This one sneaks in like a tiny weed in the crack of pavement, easy to walk past, not noticing it at all. But this weed grows so quickly that the next time you look, it's grown so large it can move the pavement itself. Be on the lookout. If you don't feel it now, you will soon. We all will.

The Truth

In the delivery of your work, you're used to being an all-star. You're an expert because you've got hard-won expertise. Let me be blunt. You're used to being *perfect*.

Quick responses from clients. Thank-yous for amazing meetings. High client survey scores. Team members vying to work with you. Awards, accolades...awesomeness. All that feedback trains your brain to expect it. Every time. Looking good externally. Looking good internally. You're always looking good.

But then there are growth activities. Let's say you want to reach out to someone you don't know well. Your doubt kicks in. Do they want this content? Did I phrase this the way they want? Will I get a quick, positive response? Do they even like me?

All these fears of looking bad have their root in the fear of rejection. The fear of looking bad is a step toward deep, scary things like not being needed, being rejected, and being abandoned. Here's the truth:

You're rarely rejected in the Doing of the Work, and you need to get used to rejection in Winning the Work.

Rejection is part of the deal. You *have* to get used to it or you won't succeed.

You won't always win the work you want. You won't always get the response you want. Sometimes, you won't get a response at all. If you're going to create value where there wasn't value before, you should expect these things to happen. They're fine. In fact, *they're good*. They mean you're pushing yourself to create value and be helpful.

Beating this lie is all about having realistic expectations. Expect you won't win every piece of work. Expect not everyone will accept your offers to attend your events. Expect you'll send thoughtful, helpful notes to clients where you worried over every word and sometimes they won't respond at all. Expect you'll have some amazing conversations at conferences and in meetings and then all of a sudden, you can't get a response. Expect all this and more!

I know this all sounds negative, but if you expect less, you'll feel better when something does happen. Some say that Happiness = Reality – Expectations. Think about how that equation will look if you apply your perfectionist Doing the Work expectations when Winning the Work. Not good! Lowering your expectations when Winning the Work will help you keep going so you can make positive progress.

Positive progress is your key to success, and here's the mindset to keep you moving.

The Solution

First, accept that you sometimes fear looking bad. Take another scan at that list above. The fear of looking bad sneaks in our minds in early relationships by causing us to worry about how to reach out. And it impacts deep relationships by causing us to pause, especially when introducing something new like a hot topic or recently hired expert. Or when revisiting something we think we're supposed to know but forgot.

Next, know what the fear of looking bad loves and hates. The fear of looking bad loves a little doubt. Doubt fertilizes this lie, helping it grow. It'll think of a way to cause you to pause, then grow it, fooling you to turn moments to hours and hours to days. And days of delays create a complete stop.

The fear of looking bad dislikes action, hates momentum, and absolutely abhors acceleration.

You'll push the fear out with action. Use action to gain momentum, then pick up the pace once you have it. Your fear will go away, finding someone else weaker to delay. Keep this mantra in mind:

Think 10x, not 1x.

1x thinking is rooted in "I have to be perfect this one time" and "I *need* the response I want to this exact thing." 10x thinking means "If I add value ten times, something will resonate at some point."

1x thinking means needing to write something with 100 percent certainty it'll land perfectly. 10x thinking means if you always have the other person's best interests in mind, they'll feel your true intent and your wording doesn't have to be absolutely perfect.

1x thinking grades a 100 percent response rate as great. 10x thinking grades *any* response is great, expecting nothing from any particular outreach.

You can use 10x thinking with a person in mind, expecting to reach out ten times with helpfulness over a longer period of time, like a year, guessing a few offers will resonate. And you can use 10x thinking with a time in mind, like inviting ten clients to an event, guessing a few people might be interested and available.

If you think you have to get a response to an email, you'll overthink it, maybe not sending anything at all. But if you think you'll reach out whenever you have something that might be helpful, you'll add tons of value over time and brand yourself as a helpful resource.

If you think a topic has to hit the bullseye before bringing it up, you'll hesitate. But if you bring up all the topics that *might* be helpful, letting the client determine what's relevant, they'll realize you're their secret weapon, someone always striving to help them see around corners and stay on top of trends.

If you think one question needs to drive engagement, you'll question your question. But if you craft several questions that could create conversation, you'll discover what resonates and your client will thank you for the delightful dialogue.

Think 10x, not 1x. Don't expect perfection—expect nothing. Pause on this positivity:

Making more attempts is another main reason Top Performers separate themselves from everyone else.

Remember that Top Performer outlier data? How nearly every organization has outlier Top Performers that bring in 10x to 30x the revenue of average performers?

The vast majority of Top Performers become great by making more attempts. More outreaches. More offers. More connections. Top Performers get attacked by the fear of looking bad too—they just blast through it faster and more often.

Make more offers of helpfulness. You'll get more no thank-yous. You'll get more nonresponses. But you'll also get a lot more of the responses you want.

My five offers to help this week are:

1.

2.

3.

4.

5.

OK, time to close out 10x thinking with one interesting perspective: the fear of looking bad can be your biggest advantage. Right now this lie is spreading, attacking countless professionals around the world, slowing their progress and limiting their attempts to be helpful.

Always remember what the fear of looking bad loves and hates. The fear of looking bad loves a little doubt. It hates action, so take action! Create your own momentum. Then accelerate it.

As you get rid of this fear through your action, it'll go find someone else's mind to meddle in, like your competition.

You'll blast through it, then it'll go blast someone else.

Now's a good time to reflect. Which of the lies is most important for you to nix next?

Here they are again:

1. I can't do that.
2. I don't know what to do.
3. I might do it wrong.
4. I'm too busy.
5. I'm going to look bad.

Circle the one that you need to annihilate. Figure out your countermove for when it creeps back in. I guarantee it will.

Once you tackle that top lie, topple the next. And keep your guard up. These little devils will try to sneak into your synapses all the time.

We've designed several posters of the five lies and their corresponding truths that you can download to print or use as screen savers. Download them at givetogrow.info.

It's funny that sometimes, success means subtracting. Get rid of these lies to unlock your next level. And adopt the truths to stay there. Now that we've got the lies out of the way, there's much more to cover.

Start rubbing your hands together, my friends. Get a bowl of popcorn ready. We're going to take things up a notch. It's time to fill in the void we just created by removing the lies.

We're going to start building your growth system. Top Performers focus on giving. Here's how to give in ways that help everyone win.

Section Three:

The Gifts

Now that we've removed the lies from your mind, we can add the gifts you'll give others.

These are a *big deal*, because these skills are rarely taught, and beyond that, most forces in the world have short-term pressure. They'll push you to do the *wrong* things. They impel you to sell, not attract. To take, not give. To be selfish, not Otherish.

Think back to the ending of Chapter 3 and the Doing the Work versus Winning the Work table. All the Doing the Work moves create *certainty* for others. This section will show the specific Winning the Work moves that create *possibility* for others.

These next four chapters will demystify what Top Performers do. You'll learn how to use your expertise to guide clients to explore all the possible outcomes, decide what should be done, then determine the best approach to take, including choosing you.

Because all of these gifts engage the client throughout the relationship with their best interests in mind, everyone wins.

Here are the four gifts in full form:

- Focus on Engagement:
  The Gift of Attention
- Fall in Love with Their Problem:
  The Gift of Understanding
- Give Them the Experience of Working with You:
  The Gift of Wisdom
- Always Make a Recommendation:
  The Gifts of Clarity and Progress

The first part of each title is your priority, and the second is the gift the client will receive.

I can't say it enough—these mindsets create wins for all involved.

And when everyone involved wins, you win too.

Chapter 12

Focus on Engagement

The biggest "sale" of my life was a purchase. My wife, Becky, and I spent almost fifteen years trying to buy our dream property—twelve acres in the heart of Atlanta, including a seven-acre pasture in the backyard.

We wanted this in-town farm to let our daughters be around horses every day, let Becky help kids with disabilities through equine therapy, and let me see it all in a super-cool eighty-year-old historical home resting in a nest of nature. After all that work growing BIG and finally closing on the house, I felt it was the most important transaction of my life. It meant *family* to me, and that meant a lot.

I wanted to improve the basement right after moving in. It had gone through a 1980s remodel and didn't fit the historical style of the home. My vision: turn it into a game room with a 1930s farmhouse feel to match the time period the home was designed and built in. After chasing the home for fifteen years, this was *really* important to me, so I wanted to get the very best expert to guide us. I did my research and found several architects who could work.

My first outreach was to a firm called Historical Concepts, and Andrew Cogar, one of their studio leaders, called me the next day. I moved things around to meet him a few days after that. I wasn't sure what to expect, and at the same time, I couldn't wait.

Knock knock: Andrew arrived. After some brief introductions, he mentioned he'd love to start with our goals and desires for the project and that if we started there, he'd be able to sketch out some ideas for how we could proceed. I liked the approach, so he led me with great questions including how we even found this hidden gem, how much we knew about its famous architect Philip T. Shutze, and what we wanted to accomplish with the project.

The talk was energizing. He sprinkled in insights about him being their firm's Shutze expert. He shared the kinds of things they learned working on other 1930s Shutze homes. He shared results of the research he had done on our home through the Atlanta History Center. He even knew Elizabeth Dowling, who I considered a rock star because she wrote the definitive book on Shutze.

And the basement! We talked about our family's love of games and entertainment, with Andrew expanding my thinking about what could be designed. He pulled out his notebook and started sketching, our vague ideas taking shape. What Andrew did in that moment was so simple and so powerful: *he just started doing the work and engaged with me as he went.*

As Andrew was leaving, he spent a minute or two covering some things he had brought, including over fifty hand-selected photographs from prior projects. We looked at a few that connected to our conversation, skipping the rest. He left with several to-dos, including sending some Shutze articles I hadn't yet found and introducing me to a landscape architect I wanted to call that day.

I waved goodbye as Andrew drove off, thinking the rest of the day would be boring compared to our conversation. I pulled out my phone. *Tick. Tick. Tick.* I crossed off the to-dos I had set up to call the other architects. Andrew was the guy for me.

Fast-forward years later and I'm a raving fan of Andrew and Historical Concepts. Their work was strong, and their passion for our project was even stronger. We even partnered to host a "home homecoming" where we invited over thirty family members of the home's prior owners to return and tell their stories in the basement we designed together. It was pure magic. Andrew and his team's work were a big part of it, with Andrew even home brewing a special Home Homecoming batch of beer. Talk about exceeding expectations! And since then, we've hosted hundreds of events in that basement, creating thousands of memories. The one choice to use Andrew has given our family a dividend of memories that'll last throughout our lifetimes.

And it all started with the perfect introductory meeting.[6] The rest of this chapter will decode why it was so great, starting with the long version of this chapter title and detailing the benefit to you.

Focus on your client's engagement so you can interact with the client in a way they love and they'd love to continue.

Give them the Gift of Attention.

---

6 I had a hoot interviewing Andrew on my *Real Relationships, Real Revenue* podcast. He talked about how they won a huge project spending the entire pitch talking about the chicken coop design. Amazing. Link at givetogrow.info.

What Most Professionals Do

Notice what this title does not say: focus on the amount of your content you can cover. Here's the most common killer of development meetings:

1. Choose the content you *think* the client wants to cover, instead of being ready to flex to their priorities.
2. Determine the amount of content you can cover if you pack the entire time with you talking, which is usually far too much. Sixty-two slides in sixty minutes? Talk! Talk! Talk!
3. Mentally rehearse each point, optimizing for the volume of information you'll convey, instead of how you'll engage the client on the key points.
4. Go into the meeting with this mindset, having prepared to talk too much, too fast, and leave little room for an enjoyable conversation between human beings.

This is sadly normal. It's focusing on filibuster, and the grade will be an F.

Focusing on engagement is a powerful differentiator.

Andrew could have started the meeting talking about his firm, their accolades, how they approach projects, or a million other things about *them*. Instead he started with me and my needs, and then he led the conversation so that those were always the focus.

As you read this chapter, notice that each section aligns with one question you can keep in mind when you're preparing to meet with and are meeting with clients: What's next to focus engagement?

Keep that question in focus and you'll accomplish a lot more. Now let's talk about what the client gets.

Guess what researcher Ohtsubo Yohsuke found was the number one correlation to intimacy? *Attention*. He and his colleagues even named their 2014 study "It's the Attention That Counts."

Showing someone attention is one of the most meaningful things you can do.

Attention builds trust. It conveys caring. It deepens relationships. Focusing on engaging the client is showing attention. It's focusing on *them*.

People in great relationships have conversations, not one-way filibusters. Say you're meeting with an old friend for lunch to catch up and have fun. Would you show up with a seventy-two-slide PowerPoint marching them through a predefined script of what's going on at work and home? ("And on slide twelve you'll see a photo of our new Winnebago!") You might pull something from your bag to show them. Or you might show a single photo from your phone or draw something on a napkin.

Conversations with your clients should be similar to how you'd treat a friend: an enjoyable and productive two-way conversation, where each side emerges a little more energized and a little better off.

Andrew did it with me, I knew exactly what he was doing, *and it felt great*. Remember the opening line to the book: I wake up every morning looking to help my friends succeed, and some of them just happen to be clients. Isn't it funny that success with clients is just treating them like you'd treat a friend?

Let's break down focusing on engagement with some science and steps. Here's how to structure your meetings with the perfect beginning, middle, and end.

Set Yourself Up for Success with a Clear Meeting Frame

Most professionals do a great job of framing meetings when Doing the Work, but for some reason they shy away from framing meetings when Winning the Work.

Here's the usual Doing the Work framing:

> Hey everyone, we've only got thirty minutes and we've got four big decisions to make so that we can get the analysis finalized by Tuesday. We've got these listed out here on the screen— sound good to dive right in?

This is a clear frame. We know what our finish line is, what success looks like, and we're all marching forward as a team.

If anything is said at all, here's the usual Winning the Work version:

> Hey, I'm so glad Lisa suggested we should meet. Should I jump in and tell you a little about what we do?

Or worse yet:

Hey Yohei, we're glad we can meet today. Hey, I'm curious, what keeps you up at night?

These last two examples have no frame at all. The decision-maker is sitting there thinking, "Why am I here?" They're thinking about everything else they have to do and how this meeting is going to be a waste of time. Smells like a sales pitch.

Here's a better frame in the context of Winning the Work:

> Hey Yiannis, I'm excited Alexa thinks we might be able to work together someday. We'd love to use this meeting to find an investment we can make in your success. What if we spend about twenty minutes learning your priorities? We've done a ton of research on your organization, including _____, _____, and _____, and have some questions to guide us.
>
> Then we could leave ten minutes at the end to think through an investment we could make that aligns with whatever priorities you share.
>
> For example, we were tentatively thinking it could be valuable for us to analyze your _____ data to see _____, but our conversation might reveal something better. How's that sound?

Bam! That framing takes less than thirty seconds to say, and in that time you've already differentiated yourself. The decision-maker is all ears. No matter what happens, you'll both win. If they like your frame, they're leaning in with curiosity. If they want to change your frame to something else they'd rather focus on, you can give them what they want.

When you use clear meeting frames at the start, everyone works together to accomplish the shared goal.

You'll win your meetings by how you set them up in the first five minutes, not in the last five minutes scrambling with some random suggestions. Most people hope and pray something meaningful will come up in a meeting. Instead, focus on how you start meetings, because that will steer everyone involved to *find* what's meaningful.

Drive Engagement in the Meeting

After you've started the meeting, your next priority is giving the client what they need, and that means reading the room. Your natural inclination is going to be using your technical skills to solve everything. That hammer is always looking for a nail. But many times, the client needs something very different.

Deliver the Support Needed

There are three main things clients might need from you in a given interaction: technical advice, emotional support, and strategic ideas.

Each of these is a completely different mode of support. The win is switching to the right mode at the right time. Here's a little more detail on each mode:

Technical advice is easy—we're almost always ready to support using our big brains and experience. Like Andrew did, just start Doing the Work! Ask: How far can I go in the time I have?

- **Emotional support is very different.** Here, the client isn't looking for answers; they're looking for someone to *listen* to them, maybe about how hard things are or something they need to share in a safe space. Ask: How can I show I'm listening with empathy?

- **Strategic ideas are exciting.** You are helping the client think through how to approach an important issue. These could be things you can be hired for or things you can't. Ask: How can I use the breadth of my experience to explore all the possibilities?

You can add a lot of value simply because you're an external partner. That *might* be related to your technical skills, but you can also be helpful emotionally and with your big ideas. Being an outsider creates a safe zone with your clients, giving you the opportunity to advise and support them far beyond your technical expertise.

Being flexible to discuss their needs is more powerful than it seems. I already mentioned Ohtsubo's research that found the top driver of intimacy is attention. The paper's name itself caught mine: "It's the Attention That Counts: Interpersonal Attention Fosters Intimacy." He summarized his team's work with this simple truth:

> These studies consistently showed that the participants increased their intimacy with a partner when they received attention from the partner.

Determining what they need and flexing to that shows attention. It conveys caring. You're treating your client like you'd treat a close friend.

Andrew did this for me in our meeting, swiftly switching between all three modes. The epic fifteen-year journey to purchase our home was meaningful to me, and I knew that as a lover and creator of spaces, he would get it more than most. He listened and let me tell the entire story, with us bonding on every setback and solution I shared.

The more deeply someone shares with you, the more they want to use you. Read the room as you enter it so you can toggle to the right mode of support. Be a friend.

During every meeting, just ask yourself this simple question: Do they need help or a hug?

Find Commonalities

Once you figure out the best mode of support, you'll want to find commonalities because commonalities correspond to liking. And the literature shows that when someone likes someone, they say yes to them more often and have a higher likelihood of buying from them. Studies of doctors even found they spend significantly more time educating patients they like. There's a lot to like about liking!

You'll want to search for shared bonds beyond just the technical work. Commonalities can be anything from dealing with similar headwinds to wanting to explore the same vacation spots. The more specific, the better—uncommon commonalities are stronger.

It's up to you to find and reinforce things you have in common with others. These can be anything professional or personal, hirable or human.

For a professional example, maybe you both like Dan Pink books, are excited about the same business trends, or worked with some of the same people in the past. For a personal example, maybe you both want to hike the Tour du Mont Blanc in France someday, make custom candles from scratch, or enjoy creating fancy cocktails with fun ingredients like fresh watermelon juice.

People make the mistake of thinking commonalities are about where you've come from. Those can work, but I've found commonalities about where you're *going* are even stronger. That makes me happy, because it means everyone can dial up their commonality game.

Having a commonality about the life you're interested in creating makes it all the more powerful to share what you're learning, whether it's brainstorming with someone about a new business framework or a clever name for that fancy cocktail you've jointly perfected. (We all know that finding the perfect name for your artisan watermelon margarita is important!) In Andrew's initial meeting, we bonded over a dozen things outside the work: design philosophies, games, running businesses, and even Andrew's passion for brewing his own beer.

Celebrate Progress

Let's take another step: everyone loves making progress!

The Progress Principle is one of the most important mental frameworks in the human mind. Researchers Teresa Amabile and Steven Kramer studied tens of thousands of knowledge workers and found one thing correlated to both productivity and happiness: people that celebrated incremental progress.

Ever been in a meeting and you don't know why you're there? It's horrible. You don't know what progress to make because you don't know what the goal is. You're sitting there thinking about anything except what's being discussed. *Why am I here? How did I get here? Are the in-laws really staying for a full week next month?*

But with your mutually agreed-upon framework as the finish line, you can call out small victories as you make them—sort of a micro-Progress Principle! For example:

> Wow, we're only twenty-three minutes in and we've already decided on a valuable investment we can make in your success. We're way ahead of schedule. Should we shift to talking through specific steps, like who we should work with on collecting the data, when we should meet again, who should be in the readout, and things like that?

Micro-bam! These little phrases not only celebrate your progress but also convey that you're a productive team making progress together. This is a game changer because celebrating incremental progress will get you more incremental progress.

The Power of Humor

There's one last thing to focus on to drive engagement in meetings: have a little fun.

Here's a quote from a study led by Nale Lehmann-Willenbrock:

> One of the most fundamental tools for successful human interaction is humor. In a business context, successful use of humor...can go beyond individual liking to create positive behaviors such as questions, new ideas, praise, etc.

You know how sports teams goof around a lot? They do everything from pulling pranks on each other to having fun ways of celebrating a home run or goal, like wearing ridiculous hats or orchestrating crazy end zone dances. This is more important than it appears.

The game of growth is like pro-level sports, with each person putting more pressure on themselves than they let on. Buying can be stressful on clients because their name is on the line. And creating a buy is stressful on you because so much is at stake. You can increase your performance by decreasing stress, and humor is the best way to do it.

Think through how you can inject a little levity into your meetings. Andrew did this throughout his meeting— we had fun thinking through the games we might add in the basement, joking about bad contractors, and sharing our favorite poorly designed homes.

Our clients have done everything from just noticing and mentioning in-meeting funny moments all the way to creating handmade funny awards to give out at the end of a project. Get with your team and figure out how to dial up the fun in your client interactions. It's fun to have fun!

End the Meeting Perfectly

It's time to end this chapter with how to end your
meetings based on the mental heuristic the Peak–End
Rule, which was validated by all-star researcher
Daniel Kahneman. It says we tend to remember the
peak of an experience and the final ending more
than anything else. Your closing should reinforce both,
and in a specific order.

Every meeting should end with recapping the next steps,
but the next steps shouldn't be your *final* ending.
Even if the next step is exciting, recapping who's going
to do what by when can be a little dry, especially
after you already covered it.

You want to end meetings on a higher emotional note,
because it's what people will remember. Positive emotional moments convey energy and linger longer. That's
why we recommend closing with both in this exact order:
the Practical Close, then the Emotional Close.[7]

As you wrap every meeting, start with the Practical
Close: next steps including who will do what by when.
And when it's true, get some Progress Principle points
by mentioning you got more done than expected.

---

7 I learned these exact words from Pat Quinn, an exceptional speech coach.
My interview with him on our *Real Relationships, Real Revenue* podcast is
one of our most listened to ever, with an average listen rate of over 100 percent,
meaning the average person listens more than once. Link at givetogrow.info.

Then you'll share the high emotional point that occurred in the meeting as you all sign off or leave the room. To do this, make a mental note of when people got the most excited, laughed the most, or shared a great story. Examples might be the client sharing they're excited about their family trip next week to an African safari, a group belly laugh about something that happened in the meeting, or when one person told a great story about their team going to Oktoberfest last year.

Right after you all agree on the Practical Close and right before you all leave the meeting, finish with the Emotional Close. Here's an example:

> Goetz, have a great time on safari with your family! You've been working hard, and I know it'll be awesome to unplug. Can't wait to hear about it when we talk in a month!

There you go, the perfect closing. Practicality and progress. Check. Empathy and emotional bonding. Check. The Peak–End Rule is powerful.

Now that we've closed out how to close a meeting, it's time to close out this chapter on focusing on engagement.

We got a lot done together, more than I even expected. Let's celebrate our incremental progress!

Want to come over to my basement to play some games? I'll make a fancy cocktail with a clever name. That would be some Low-Hanging Watermelon!

Chapter 13

Fall in Love with Their Problem

I failed miserably in a meeting a few years ago. It was a *big* miss. I'd been working with a prospect for over five years, trying to find the right time to help her organization. We both enjoyed staying in touch, and I just knew the right time would come at some point.

The moment finally came, and fast: a new boss with a mandate to grow. Yes! My friend reached out, pitched an introductory meeting with all three of us, perfectly positioning the meeting for success. She told me to show up, "do my thing," and we'd be off to the races.

We started the video conference with the perfect meeting frame, including some smiles and stories. (Chapter 12 would be proud.) I was ready to ask the new boss questions to see what her priorities were when I made the worst mistake of them all: I fell for the ego trap. My friend, trying to be helpful, had said, "Mo, tell her about all the clients you work with." I did, and it's an impressive list. I felt myself proudly reflecting back on how far we'd come in the fifteen-plus years we'd been building the business to that point.

Then another: "Mo, tell her about all your modules in your GrowBIG training and how it teaches all the things someone needs to be great at growth!" I was happy to answer that one, too. Our system is comprehensive, and it's fun to talk about all the concepts we cover. I especially light up talking about the science underneath everything we teach.

One after the other, my friend kept asking questions. She knew their company and our content because it had helped her so much, so I felt like I had a sherpa guiding us, one step at a time. It was glorious! I had so much fun talking about the impact we have and how we accomplish so much with our clients. Measurable results. Success stories. Personal impact. We covered it all. We crammed so much in that we went a few minutes over when the boss had to run to another call. We decided to email to get another time to talk.

It was so great...until it wasn't. The call ended and I looked down at my notes. That's when I realized I had no notes. It was a blank page. Nothing. I didn't know a thing about her. I never asked one question. Oh man. I realized I fell into a trap. Ego. Pride. I talked about myself and BIG the entire time.

Guess how many meetings we had after that? None. I messed the whole thing up.

I'll never forget that meeting. When I was asked to talk about myself, I should have given a thirty-second overview and turned the focus back on her. I didn't ask her about her priorities. I didn't ask anything.

There's a slew of reasons why it's easy to focus on yourself ahead of the client. The trap in that case was my ego, but a lot of other things can happen, so let's broaden our view.

Almost every force inside your organization is pushing you to fall in love with yourself and your stuff. Your new marketing efforts. Your people. Your solutions. We need more cross-selling! We brought in a new expert and need to introduce her to our clients! We have a new solution, including an awesome PowerPoint to describe it!

All of this focus and language is a powerful social vector, one that will push you to be selfish over Otherish and to put the spotlight on yourself, your team, and your organization over your clients. Don't do it! Top Performers fall in love with their clients' problems, not their own solutions.

Here's the long version of this chapter title:

Fall in love with their problem so you can find a meaningful way to help them.

And here's the key to doing that: focus on asking questions and understanding their answers.

Clients feel when they're being sold to. And they also feel when someone's digging in and trying to understand the problem. How you approach asking questions and listening in your meetings is one of the biggest differentiators you can have.

This chapter is going to show how to do this the right way. It's notable that the fastest way for you to get hired is to talk about them. As you learn in this chapter, pay attention to how everything aligns with one key question: What do I need next to be able to paraphrase their problem back to them and test my understanding of the situation?

By doing this, you're giving them the Gift of Understanding, and it's a golden gift. It sends a strong message. *I get you. I see you. I understand you.* Keeping the Gift of Understanding in mind will keep you from falling into the trap of talking about yourself. It'll guide you to the next right question. And it'll show the client that you're different and truly trying to help. Understanding is your outcome and the best path to get there is with well-designed questions.

Let this guide you during your meetings: What should I ask next to understand their priorities in their own words?

Design Your Initial Questions to Be Enjoyable to Answer

The pleasure center of the brain is powerful. It's firing when we're eating great food or drinking a good cup of coffee, and asking your questions in a specific way can light up the pleasure center of someone else's mind. This is powerful—you can literally give your client a high by asking your questions in the right way.

Diana Tamir and her research teams tell us how to do this by using functional MRI machines to measure blood oxygenation in the brain. Her work tells us precisely when someone's pleasure center is firing. There's so much to her work, but the main thing you need to remember is that the pleasure center lights up when someone is answering questions from their own personal perspective, sharing things only they know.

You've heard people say that "people love talking about themselves." That might be true, but we can be more precise now that we know the science.

People love sharing their personal perspective.

Your best questions are going to make it clear you want someone's personal perspective on something— that's what'll get their pleasure center firing and give them a high. Not only will they be enjoying every moment, but you'll be able to learn what you need to help them succeed, falling in love with their problem.

Here is an example:

> Hey Katrina, this economy is crazy, and everyone has an opinion on what's happening. You have a unique perspective as CFO of a multinational retailer. What's your take on where things are headed?

Notice the nuance. The question makes it clear we're asking for something only Katrina knows. Imagine her response—she might answer for five or ten minutes straight. She'll be on a high and you'll be learning with every word. Win-win!

I am going to ask my client about their priorities with this question...

Be Supportive as You Listen

You want to add supportive comments as others share their perspectives. This has benefits that pay off right away and down the road. Evan Kleiman shared this quote in one research study he and his team led:

> We found that when people received supportive reactions after sharing something about themselves during the social interaction, this resulted in immediate positivity and a more positive memory of the event (remembered enjoyment and positive emotions) one week later.

So ask, listen, and support. Sometimes it's nothing more than "Wow, that must be tough seeing things in the organization before others do." Or "I'm hopeful people will listen next time." Even small reactions can make a big difference.

Asking questions and being supportive is easy to understand but hard to do because we want to be talking about our own awesome expertise.

Remember that your own pleasure center is trying to hijack your actions! That was my mistake in that meeting I described. I fell for the ego trap where, over and over, I was sharing my own personal perspective on how our approach works, how we've helped clients succeed so much, and how enjoyable it was for me to be a part of it. I was blinded by being on such a pleasure center high that I couldn't see anything else. And because of that, I never saw another meeting with that prospect again.

Resist the urge to talk about yourself too much. It's not about you yet. Focus on them first. You'll get to talk about yourself soon enough, and with much more precision than if you start with you.

Focus on Follow-Up Questions for Even More Benefits

But wait, there's more! Another benefit of personal perspective questions is that it makes you more likable. In a meta-review, Nancy Collins and team's research found that self-disclosure had powerful effects on relationships. They found three forces pulling together create a powerful likability flywheel effect:

1. More intimate disclosure correlates to more liking;
2. People disclose more later to those they initially like; and
3. People like others more after they disclose to them.

Wow, that's a lot of *mores*.

Now, guess what type of questions highly correlate to liking? Follow-up questions.

You'll want to prepare with questions that give people an opportunity to share their perspective, but you'll want to be looking for moments when the client really lights up, where they display passion. When that happens, ask some version of this.

Here are the three magic words to base your follow-up questions on: "Tell me more."

Let's build off the questions above, assuming the initial questions springboard into personal perspective answers:

> Katrina, that's super interesting that you think the Fed's interest rate policy is going to change. Why do you think that will happen?

Imagine a client meeting where the client passionately talks 80 percent of the time. They're into it, their pleasure center firing like they just drank a quadruple espresso. And what do they think about you? They feel your caring. That you're trying. That you're different from the other professionals they've met. All this creates a great experience for them and a long-term relationship advantage for you.

Showcase Your Expertise with Advanced Questions

Are you curious about what can take your questions to another level? The answer is...curiosity. There are three reasons why:

- Curiosity is an intrinsic motivator. Intrinsic motivations are powerful because you don't need a reward to want to move forward. Curiosity is the motivation itself.
- Curiosity creates arousal, excitement, and awareness in the mind. People are dialed in when curious.
- Curiosity triggers better memory of facts and figures.

Creating curiosity about how you can help them is the most effective way to talk about yourself. That's because seeding curiosity throughout the conversation will eventually turn the conversation back to you in a way the client will love, because they're motivated and in control, steering the conversation toward the highest value. And they'll remember what they hear.

Here's an example, modifying the simpler version of the same question presented earlier in the chapter. I've highlighted the addition designed to create curiosity: ➜

Hey Katrina, this economy is crazy, and everyone has an opinion on what's happening. We've got some "hot off the press" survey results on what other CFOs are thinking, and the results are different than what we expected. But I'm interested in your unique perspective as CFO of a major multinational retailer. What's your take on where things are headed?

If I ask the same question and add an item about our work, I will say...

Pro Tip: Before the meeting, do your research to design great questions. Focus on what will create curiosity about you and what will create a high for them. Then, in the meeting, see what resonates and dig in deep. They'll like the experience, and more importantly, they'll like you.

You'll find that incorporating some curiosity into your questions will create interest. Then, when the time is right, the client will turn the focus back on you, which I'll cover in a moment. But first, you've got to give them the Gift of Understanding, and there's a specific way to give it.

We've developed a list of over fifty go-to questions you can download at givetogrow.info.

Paraphrasing Earns You the Right to Continue

Your goal throughout all this is paraphrasing your clients' priorities in their own words.

This is because there's an invisible gate between you and your next step: *the client needs to know you get it*. This doesn't happen through head nods, active listening, or mental telepathy. You have to use your words for them to get that you get it. The Gift of Understanding has to be said to be received.

Pulling through our sample conversation:

> Katrina, let me see if I've got this right. You think this recession is going to last a lot longer than everyone else, which is going to put pressure on your cost structure, and you're worried about getting ahead of it.

Paraphrasing back seems so straightforward that some people want to skip it. Don't. It might be obvious to you that you "get it," but it's not obvious to the client until they hear you say it. Some worry they might not paraphrase things perfectly, but being perfect isn't the point. Testing your understanding is. You win whether you're perfect or far from it.

If the prospect agrees with you, you win.

> That's exactly right, Mo! And my job is on the line to make this happen soon.

And you also win if the client tweaks your message, because you get even more clarity on what they need.

> I wouldn't quite use the word "worried," Mo, but I would agree we need to focus on removing cost from the entire enterprise, that we need to do it soon, and we need to do it in a way that impacts both the P&L statement and balance sheet.

Remember this:

Paraphrasing back is the only way the prospect knows you get their situation. Full stop.

It feels great for them to be understood, and paraphrasing is your path to giving them that feeling. You can paraphrase small things as you go along and recap important themes near the end of the meeting. Both are important, and both work. We'll talk more about making recommendations later, but for now, practice paraphrasing until you're a pro. It's an important skill in its own right.

How to Know When It's Your Turn

Two things will tell you it's your turn. First, the client might feel enough curiosity that they turn the light back on you:

> Hey Mo, what was interesting about that survey you mentioned a few minutes ago?

Talking about yourself works best when it's the client's idea. If they ask you a question, make sure you paraphrase back what you heard first:

Oh sure, I can tell you all about it, including the things we found surprising. But first, let me make sure I got your perspective on your priorities right, because once we're aligned there, I can share the survey results that'll be most meaningful to you.

Remember that invisible gate: they need to get that you get it. This shows alignment and leverages curiosity even more. Everyone wins.

The second way to shift the focus to you is by prompting it yourself. If the client hasn't asked a question, you can prompt it in a way that's helpful. Right after you paraphrase back their priorities in their own words and you've both agreed you've got it right, offer to be helpful. Here's an example:

Hey Katrina, would now be a good time to share a few elements of that survey I mentioned? One insight is particularly interesting because it could help you educate the senior leadership team on the area you mentioned was important to you.

That'll get a yes every time because 1) they've already felt curiosity about the survey because you sprinkled it in beforehand; 2) you're tying it precisely to a need they shared, going straight to their priorities using their own words; and 3) you're being helpful by promising insights about something important to them. Now you can talk about yourself, your organization, and your solutions in a targeted way.

I had to choose something generic as an example of what to talk about, so I chose a survey, but you should choose whatever has the most value given the context. That could be talking through stories of how other clients have solved a problem, data you have, process steps you know work, or anything else. You'll always want to talk about yourself in specific ways that add value in their own right.

Why the Gift of Understanding Is So Powerful

Your competition is talking about themselves 70 percent of the meeting, hoping something sticks. Is that invisible overcooked spaghetti behind the client on the wall there from the last meeting they were in? You're going to get the client talking about their priorities and passions 70 percent of the meeting, finding exactly what sticks. No guessing.

You should keep asking follow-up questions to explore every aspect from their perspective. Keep asking until you fully understand the situation, sprinkling in insights of your own, until their passion dies down. Only then should you change topics. You're a detective, looking for clues of passion so you can fully understand their priorities in their own words.

Then, because the client is choosing the 30 percent of the meeting that's about you, you'll know *exactly* what they're interested in. With their needs in mind, you'll provide targeted offers of helpfulness.

Just remember your goal throughout the meeting: What should I ask next to understand their priorities in their own words? And once you have that: How can I paraphrase their priorities back to them to show them I get it? Doing this earns you the right to continue.

There's a great irony in all this work you've done to become an expert advisor and a professional. What's in your big brain is unique. Your solutions are the best there is. But the client doesn't want your broad-based knowledge that results in what feels like cookie-cutter solutions.

Clients don't want slightly modified boilerplate materials. Clients want you to tailor what you know to their unique situation.

They want your understanding. They want you to get it. They want you to fall in love with their problem.

Chapter 14

Give Them the Experience of Working with You

I still can't believe the impact one experiment had on our business. That crazy idea is now one of our most important ongoing business processes. It felt great unfurling around me as it happened, but it was even better as the opportunities came in a few short weeks after we gave it a shot. Sitting around the dinner table one night, I remember telling my wife and daughters that it was the best bet I had ever made.

BIG was small at the time, but we were starting to gain traction. I had been coaching people for a few years and seen the need for something more comprehensive and scalable. Seeing the need, I invested nearly all of our family's savings and months of my personal time into codifying the first GrowBIG training. The cost and the opportunity cost were a big bet.

We invested so much I felt like we had gone straight from a Level One to Level Ten impact in a few short months. I knew we had something powerful and had hedged my bet because a few clients wanted to hire us for the training just from seeing the original prototypes.

The feedback they gave me was meaningful—it was the first business development training course they had seen that made the long-term relationship the top priority. Those initial clients loved the training. Validation!

But then I ran into a wall. And this wall was *thick*. Not enough people were buying. And even though my original investment was paid back, I didn't have a big financial buffer, so I needed to make this work.

I was getting plenty of new introductions. Some were from years of investing in other people's success. Others were referrals from leaders sponsoring the initial successful trainings. The beginnings of those calls were going great. I was focusing on engagement and falling in love with each prospect's problems. Even better, most wanted to grow more quickly and give their professionals a common playbook for everyone to leverage together, so I was finding the fit strong with most of the meetings.

That's where I crashed into the wall. I'd describe the training, carefully aligning the outcomes I could give them to their priorities and their words. But no one was buying. And the money was running out.

Around this time, I remember Becky and I going out for a dinner celebration with another couple. The sommelier was talking about how great a particular wine was, but we weren't biting. Money was too tight. It was higher than we wanted to spend, which I'm sure he picked up by the silent stares we all gave each other as he was talking about it.

Everything changed when he brought us each a surprise taste. It was small, but we swirled, sniffed, and savored every drop. He could've talked for another twenty minutes, but it wasn't as persuasive as that twenty-second taste. We bought the bottle and loved it.

That was my a-ha moment. A taste is more powerful than a talk. I needed to give people a taste of the training, even if it was at no cost. Because I had a "training" solution, people were bucketing our training into what they had experienced before, which most people told me wasn't great. My talking about how ours is different just wasn't working—they had to *experience* it to feel the difference. They needed a taste!

So I worked with our team to design a "public" version of our GrowBIG training where a single person or small group could sign up, and we'd jigsaw-puzzle a dynamic class out of everyone who could attend.

This one move had a myriad of positive effects. I could gift the course to prospects or friends to let them try it out, which moved people through the buying process. I could let our early clients pay to send new hires through the full training instead of waiting a year or more until they had a sizable group, which sped up buying. And I could invest in my Strategic Partner relationships, letting them attend at no charge, which helped them grow their businesses and let them talk about their experience with firsthand examples to hundreds of prospects.

This led me to common wisdom that's uncommonly acted upon:

Hearing about something isn't nearly as compelling as experiencing it.

Years later, thousands of people have been positively impacted through our public GrowBIG trainings, and those thousands of public trainees have led to tens of thousands impacted with trainings tailored just for their company, which is most of what we do.

I'm not sure what our growth would have been like without this move, but it doesn't take actuarial modeling to know it would be lower. A *lot* lower. That bottle of wine was one of the best investments I ever made.

Let's switch back to you. One thing will correlate to how fast you'll grow more than anything else: how much value you provide clients before they choose you.

You can add value in lots of ways. Our first two mindsets add a lot of value in their own right: focus on engagement and fall in love with their problem. These will give your clients a wonderful experience, one that magnetically attracts them to wanting to work with you. They feel your attention. They know you understand.

But you can't stop there. To have a big impact, clients need to hire you and pay you money. Get comfortable with this. It's an important part of the value exchange, and you're worthy of charging for your value.

That leads us to a longer version of this chapter's title:

Give them the experience of working with you so that hiring you is a safe and simple next step.

What most professionals do is talk about what it's like to work with them: offering client success stories, sample client logos, project plans, testimonials, and more. This is like hearing about how great the expensive wine is from the sommelier. It's still risky to buy the bottle. But after a taste? Getting that taste makes buying the bottle a safe and simple next step. And you know how it goes. Once you buy that first bottle, you're going for more.

Talking about what you do isn't differentiating. Your competitors have a proven process, a great client list, and super success stories. I guarantee their materials look as good as yours. To the client, it all sounds the same.

But letting a client experience what you do *is* differentiating. Just making an investment will separate you from those that don't, but far beyond that, experiencing you in action will make purchasing your services safe and a simple next step.

So here's the question you can keep in mind during every client interaction: How can I let this client experience what we're talking about?

You'll want to invest in a way the client is excited about and says yes to. And you'll also want to invest in ways that pay off for you and your teams. Making it work for everyone is where the magic is. Let's make some magic.

Invest in Client Success with a Give to Get

Think about what most professionals do. They try to go straight from the introduction of themselves, another expert, or a new offering directly to getting hired—the Big Win. But your Big Win is a big risk for them! Hearing about how great you are without experiencing you in action is high stakes. That's why most introductions don't result in anything; the risk gap is too big between the introduction and a signed contract.

Give to Grow is a mindset, something that will guide your growth for decades. A Give to Get is a discrete offer of help, almost like a small project performed at no charge as an investment in the client relationship. It drives specific value, an outcome you can discuss and document. It has an end date. It involves specific people.

All great Give to Gets have three things in common:

1. They have immense value, so the client wants to say yes.
2. They're worth the effort for you.
3. They lead to a significant next step.

You can think of Give to Gets as an important step from introducing something new to getting hired. Here's the model to have in mind.

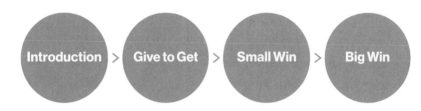

You can get a higher success rate with lower risk by offering an investment in their success, a Give to Get. Sometimes you'll have to offer multiple Give to Gets to get a single yes. Sometimes, you'll perform multiple Give to Gets to get one Small or Big Win. It's not always linear, but it is always deepening the relationship and creating momentum.

And while this chapter is mostly about creating initial momentum with a Give to Get, don't discount the power of designing a strong Small Win. Remember those four small projects I was asked to pitch the CHRO in the opening chapter? A year later, two of those Small Wins became Big Wins, both being about the size of the original engagement, which you might remember had been the largest project our office had landed that year. This was huge! But it gets even better. Another one of those Small Wins became the largest global consulting project my firm had ever been hired to do!

Great Give to Get Examples

Time for some examples. Let's start with what *isn't* a Give to Get:

- Sending someone a thought piece like a video link, article, or book is not a Give to Get. Those are great for staying at the top of their mind, but the client didn't get to experience your expertise.
- A fee concession is not a Give to Get—it's negotiation. The client didn't get to experience your expertise.
- Providing an introduction to someone else when you're not present is not a Give to Get for the same reason as the previous two examples. These are great things to do, but it doesn't give the client the experience of working with you.

Let's explore that first example, because it's the most confusing. Say you've got a client that just received a significant promotion. Great news for you and them. And say you've read and taken personal notes on the excellent book *The First 90 Days* by Michael D. Watkins, which gives a science-based approach to designing the perfect first three months after getting a new role.

While sending them the book is helpful, it's not a Give to Get because they aren't getting a taste of the experience of working with you. Instead, let's say you meet them for a one-hour coffee meeting, give them the book and your notes, then discuss your guidance on what they should prioritize based on your deep expertise and knowledge of their organization and their function. You've double-espressoed their speed to success. It's a Give to Get because they'd get the experience of working with you: you'd naturally weave in your expertise of how things get done, what strategies could work, the order of priorities, and of course, your content knowledge and how they might benefit from working with you.

Now, let's take a second and think about what would happen after the one-hour coffee meeting. Immense goodwill. Tons of interest in what you do. Mutual understanding of how you can help each other. Lots of follow-ups on precise actions. And deep relationship-building queued for months and years to come!

With that example in mind, let's talk about other great Give to Gets. Not all of these will apply to you and your world, but having a long list will give you an idea of what's possible. Three criteria are important for great Give to Gets: they're scaled to the right size relative to the potential work you can win, they're valuable for the client so they'll want them, and they naturally lead to the next step. Here are some examples:

- **Blue Sky Days,** where you have various experts talk to the client about the trends they're seeing in their discipline, applying what they're learning to the client's situation. A Small Win next step might be deeper dives in the most important topics.

- **Proposal Co-Creation,** where you work with the client to create the perfect project plan. A Small Win next step might be talking through the plan with decision-makers. Or maybe you can skip the Small Win and get hired in a Big Win!

- **Technical Analysis,** where you analyze something specific for the client, showcasing your expertise. A Small Win next step could be a readout of your findings with decision-makers.

- **Business Case Development,** where you model the economic and broader case for change that aligns with you getting hired. The Small Win next step might be a live readout with various decision-makers.

- **Introductions,** where you bring the client together with another client that has used you, *with you present*. Notice the key element with this: you're there to guide the discussion. Here, you'll help direct the conversation, sprinkling in your learnings and advice. That's the magic; they get to experience you, not just your client. A Small Win next step might be the Proposal Co-Creation option above.

- **Strategy Sessions,** where you lead the client through developing a strategy for something important to them. The Small Win next step might be offering a Proposal Co-Creation for a topic within your area of expertise that's important to them.

- **Benchmarking,** where you share database insights you have or go deeper and actually show how a client compares against the database. The Small Win next step might be a project that gets them closer to the goals the benchmarking reveals.

Notice the nuance in all these. The client gets an experience of working with you, the session itself is very valuable for them, and, importantly, every one of these has a high likelihood of leading to the next step. I hope your mind is spinning on what could work for you. But before we choose, let's go Pro. This is what will make your Give to Gets great.

Pro-Level Give to Gets

Someone can learn the rules of chess in five minutes, but that doesn't make them a chess master. Similarly, you can get the broad idea of Give to Gets quickly, but how you design them makes all the difference.

Here's some significant science from psychologist Robert Cialdini's research. He's easily the worldwide expert on influence, documenting the six most important components when it comes to influencing and persuading the human mind.

The first two are usually done in Give to Gets:

- **Reciprocity.** We want to repay those that give to us. This is the gift of investment!

- **Likability.** We say yes to those we like. Here, you'll want to use your many new interactions preparing for, implementing, and following up with your Give to Gets to find things you have in common. (This has a nice tie back to Chapter 12).

Now, let's slow down a bit, because these next two levers aren't used nearly as often. As these are harder to implement, I've added a Pro Tip for each:

- **Authority.** We trust authority figures, especially in times of stress. Hiring a new professional or buying a new solution is stressful!

  Pro Tip: Bring in your most authoritative experts on your Give to Gets, especially in brand-new and very large opportunities. The higher the stakes, the higher-level the expert should be.

- **Scarcity.** We want more of what there is less of. As a professional, your most precious commodity is your time.

  Pro Tip: Don't shoot yourself in the foot by being overly nice and saying, "It's no problem at all for us to do this for you." Instead, if it's the truth, showcase your scarcity: "We can only make an investment this big in three clients this year, and we'd like you to be one of them."

Now things get even more interesting. Here are the last two levers of influence—these are rarely used before people go through our workshops, so I've included Pro Tips here too. Time to level up!

- **Social Proof.** We feel comfortable making big decisions when people around us are comfortable too. Researcher Janetta Lun summed this nicely in a study: "We determine what is correct by finding out what other people think is correct."

  Pro Tip: Ask for the decision-makers to be a part of the experience in some way. Otherwise, you won't go as far as you want as fast as you want.

- **Commitment.** We tend to continue down roads we start down. You need to make a recommendation at the end of the Give to Get. This is so important that the entire next chapter will detail how to do this well.

  Pro Tip: More to come, but for now, know this: your client *wants* you to recommend the next step at the end of this one. Spend as much time thinking about your recommendation as you spend thinking about your content.

A lot of people ask where they should draw the line between unpaid and paid work.

You want to design the Give to Get experience in a way that you invest the minimum amount to get the maximum payoff.

Another way to think of it: invest just enough that the client sees they need you and it's a safe, simple next step to hire you. You're in control of how much you invest, so draw the line at "just enough" to get things going.

So that's how to design your Give to Gets. Here's an activity to get you going. You'll remember the six levers of influence are Reciprocity, Likability, Authority, Scarcity, Social Proof, and Commitment.

The best way to share the experience of working with me is by...

How to Offer Your Give to Gets

The investment of a Give to Get will differentiate you, and how you offer it can too. As soon as you've figured out and fallen in love with the client's problem, you'll want to offer your Give to Get. Here's how:

1. **Make the client feel special.** Remember the science of scarcity. Don't use phrases like "it's no big deal" when you offer your investment. It is a big deal, and it's appropriate for you to frame it that way.

2. **Paraphrase the client's problem.** It's important to use their priorities in their own words and not your jargon or buzzwords. Delete those from your mind and only use the client's language. This will show alignment.

3. **Anchor on value.** This is optional but powerful if you choose to do it. You'll want to mention the value of working together long term, anchoring the client on your value rather than your fees.

4. **Be transparent about the vision.** There are times this step won't make sense to do (perhaps because of cultural nuances or because it's already implied), but it's usually a good idea to say *why* you're investing. Americans are generally more blunt

about investments, while European and Asia Pacific professionals are more nuanced, so fit this to what will work for you.

5. **Offer with maximum chance of a yes.** Use this magical phrase to offer the actual Give to Get: "Would it be helpful if...?" You'll get a yes more often if you do.

Of course, we offer Give to Gets ourselves. Remember this chapter's opening story about our public training classes? We offer several a year, and it's the most frequent investment we make in our clients' and prospects' success. Here's an example of how we might make the offer at the end of an initial call:

> I've enjoyed our conversation today, Ernesto. I've got an idea. We run a public version of our workshop several times a year—would it be helpful if we had three of your top professionals attend one of those at no charge from us?

> That would let you invest in several of your high performers and let them experience our entire training to see how it could impact the Five-Year Growth Mandate you described.

> Getting everyone using the same growth playbook and system should be able to help you tap into

that $1 billion opportunity we talked through. And if it goes like we both think it will, it would be easy to get approval for a small pilot if your attendees see the fit.

We offered something similar to this to a prospective client once, and it happened to be right after we talked through the Give to Get concept itself. He blurted out, "Hey, was that a Give to Get?" I told him it sure was and asked him how it felt. He said it felt *great*.

Scale Your Efforts with a Go-To Give to Get

Here's one last give from me so you can get the most from your Give to Gets. You'll grow your impact the most with Give to Gets that scale.

First, some reconciliation. On the one hand, falling in love with the client's problems means customized investments tailored to their unique needs. That makes them feel special. But on the other hand, you want some consistency in your investments. That lets you add multiples of value because you can systematize your investments.

You can have both with a Go-To Give to Get, which is an investment you'll make the majority of the time (say, more than 60 percent of your investments). This way you'll get the benefits of scale because you'll use it often, but you'll retain the ability to be flexible for the most important opportunities.

To choose the best Go-To Give to Get, start by thinking backwards. What Big Win do you want to create more of?

Many professionals make the mistake of anchoring themselves on investments they've made in the past. Don't fall for that trap.

Instead, anchor your mind on the work you want to create demand for. Maybe it's your most profitable work. Or maybe it's the kind of work that has leverage (like if a client hires you for it, they'll likely hire you for much more). Whatever you choose, let's call that your Big Win. With that in mind, think backwards to your Small Win. Maybe it's normal to share a co-created proposal with the CFO.

Then with the Small Win in mind, design your Go-To Give to Get. It could be a specific process to co-create a proposal that wrings dozens of hours out of a two-hour session. Or package up a benchmarking database, evaluation process, whiteboarding session, or executive interview series that you can dial in efficiently.

Having one Go-To Give to Get will let you offer immense value per unit of time invested. Then, when you need to deviate from your Go-To Give to Get, go for it. No worries. Maybe there's a huge opportunity that needs a bit bigger investment or something more bespoke.

Choose this and then lean into it. Design and systematize the experience. You'll get leverage. They'll get value. And you'll both win big.

Would it be helpful if...

Remember that the things that work in Doing the Work are the exact opposites of what works in Winning the Work. When Doing the Work, you want to manage scope, optimizing utilization and profitability. In Doing the Work, it's a gotcha to give too much away.

But in Winning the Work, you *want* to give things away. You're creating demand with your hard-won expertise. You're determining exactly *what* and *how much* to give away to get to the next step.

Let's close this chapter with a reflection. Think of a few times when someone gave to you, when they helped you advance something meaningful. My mind jumps to my parents, who gave to me endlessly. I remember specifics from my childhood, like my mom patiently teaching me how to sew and my dad teaching me to improve in sports. I think of my wife, Becky, who helps me think through every scenario in life, every night.

Then a flood of scenes from outside my family comes to me. Arthur showing me how to know when a Boston butt is ready to pull off the smoker, and Dawson helping me with a better way to mark the disc while playing ultimate frisbee. And Josh mapping out the marketing plan for my first book, when I was more stressed than I could even comprehend.

We all have friends who notice a need and jump in to help us, without expecting anything in return. They help get a task done and help us get better.

It's hard to describe, but we feel different around givers. It includes gratitude and thankfulness, but it also includes an overwhelming sensation to give back to them. It always starts with a simple offer of helpfulness, and grows from there.

Whether at work or at home, the feeling is the same. We want to help others that help us. You want to be that person. You want to be the one that gives first.

Most professionals are taught that they should Get to Give. Get the contract first so you can give some value. No way.

Start with giving. Sure, it's true that givers succeed. They win more than their share. But I think the deeper truth is that givers lead more meaningful lives.

Chapter 15

Always Make a Recommendation

I don't like this advice, and I hear it often: "You always need to ask for the business!"

I know people who say this have good intentions, and I like that they're pushing for action. The theme is spot on, but the semantics are off.

I always felt this way, but after being on the receiving end of "being asked for the business" once, it really sunk in. Someone wanted us to recommend their technology to our clients, and they were promising big payouts for a referral to any client that used them. We work with prestigious organizations, so I could see why they wanted to use us as a distribution channel.

The person started the meeting with "We'd love to send you big checks" and "We'd love to meet all your clients," among several other things. I hadn't even seen their technology yet! After gagging a few times, I just had to blurt out what was happening, with an ask of my own: "Please stop saying things like that."

I'm sure they did want all those things, but I didn't want any of them. It was just too much, too fast, and I was turned off and tuned out. I'm sure this person was told they should "ask for the business" over and over. There *is* a time to ask for the business. But asking too soon isn't just ineffective, it can actually be harmful.

Here's why: There might be a hundred small steps on the path to getting hired for something significant. Asking for the business might come up in a few of them, especially in the very beginning: "It would be fun to work together someday." Or at the very end: "We need the contracts signed tomorrow to start work on Monday like we all want." But if your "ask for the business" habit is always on, it can be a big turnoff. And in some cultures, it's downright weird. (Those in the United Kingdom might think: "Well, no duh, you'd like to work with us!")

I'd say it this way...

You always need to make a recommendation.

Making a recommendation is the right thing to do, and doing it the right way helps the decision-maker. You cut through the clutter. You give clarity. You solidify your role as expert and guide.

Then, after you make the recommendation, you want to engage the client to see what they think and solicit their improvement ideas. This is more powerful than it appears because of a mental heuristic called the IKEA Effect, validated by Michael Norton from Harvard. It essentially says two things: 1) we buy into what we help create; and 2) we view our own work product as better than it is. So by engaging the client in conversation after our recommendation, we'll see where they stand and improve on the ideas, and they'll engage in the next steps.

Agreeing on what to do next gives the Gift of Progress. Everyone loves progress. Making progress is what life is all about!

In the case with the potential partner, he could have said:

> Mo, if you can share more about the skills you teach and the areas your clients struggle to implement, we can show you how others have used our tech to be successful. Then at the end of the meeting, maybe we can think through some next steps where everyone wins.

Had he done that, he would have heard more about our strong beliefs of giving first, where his tech might align, and more. Skipping too far ahead too quickly killed him before he even began.

Back to you, with the longer version of this chapter title:

You should always make a recommendation that's simple, valuable, and easy so you can help the client see what makes sense to do next.

So, here's what you can keep in mind during meetings: What's the simple, valuable, and easy next step I can recommend? Look for that. Then offer or recommend it. There's a lot more we'll cover in this chapter to help you do this comfortably and confidently, but next, I'd recommend you just keep reading.

Why and When You Should Make Recommendations

Making recommendations speeds everything up. They have scale because they permeate all aspects of the buying process from beginning to end. They have impact because they steer the process in a way that's beneficial to all. You can make recommendations at the beginning of meetings, in the middle, and especially near the end, leaving time to discuss.

Here's the problem: Most professionals shy away from making recommendations when trying to Win the Work. Maybe they're not confident. Maybe they fall in love with the content and try to cram in too much. Maybe they think it's salesy. Not so! The client is thinking of the 8 other meetings and 108 other emails they have to tackle today. Whatever decision they're making with you is just one of the countless they need to make today. To summarize:

The client wants you to make a recommendation.

You make recommendations when you Do the Work, and you should do it when you're trying to Win the Work. You're helping them by making a recommendation. You're making their life easier. It's mutually beneficial. Is my recommendation on recommendations clear enough?

Here's a bit more:

Always make a recommendation, and always leave time to discuss it.

This will be stressful at times for different reasons. Sometimes it might feel pushy. Sometimes you won't have all the content covered. That's OK. You *have* to make a recommendation.

Think of it this way. If you continue to cover content all the way to the end, the client will leave confused.

They'll thank you for all the content, but they won't have the next step, which isn't a good feeling. Being "nice" by not breaking the flow to make a recommendation isn't nice in the end.

Pro Tip: Breaking in to talk next steps is much easier if you get agreement to do it ahead of time. You might say something like this near the beginning of your meeting:

> We've got so much great content to cover today that I suspect we won't get through everything. I'd suggest transitioning to talking next steps with about fifteen minutes to go, no matter where we are in the content. How's that sound?

That thirty seconds in the beginning will gain you fifteen minutes at the end—and keep 100 percent of your momentum!

Next, let's talk about what to offer.

What to Offer: Cliffhangers

Here's the most powerful factor in getting from one meeting to the next: a cliffhanger. Think of your favorite serial TV show, especially where one episode's story leads to the next. I guarantee the writers are thinking of how they build up and orchestrate the ending more than anything else. Those last few minutes have much more leverage than a few minutes in the middle. They want you to want to watch the next episode, and right now. Attention is the asset! You can use the power of cliffhangers too, especially to build excitement and engagement for your recommended next step.

Cliffhangers add excitement to buying. They're unresolved topics that everyone is looking forward to resolving in the next interaction.

Maybe you'll dig into the data to provide insights next time you meet. Maybe the interaction is a working session to create something together. Maybe you'll be introducing a renowned expert.

You might have to offer more than one cliffhanger to make sure you get a yes on at least one. I recommend the magical phrase we used a few times: Would it be helpful if...?

Here are some examples pulling from our example CFO discussion with Katrina in Chapter 13:

- Would it be helpful if I introduced you to our global cost-takeout expert?
- Would it be helpful if we invested in your success, doing a preliminary analysis of how much cost might be removed from the enterprise?
- Would it be helpful if I introduced you to another CFO we just worked with who took 8 percent out of the organization in nine months and added $40 billion in total shareholder return?
- Would it be helpful if we got our teams together and co-created how we might approach working together?

How You Should Offer Recommendations

Three things make recommendations rock:

Make your recommendations simple, valuable, and easy.

We want something simple: it can be described in a sentence. We want something valuable: it's worth the investment of time and money. And we want something easy: the decision can be made quickly.

Include those in your recommendations and you'll get the next meeting. That's the cliffhanger.

Let's broaden our focus. In general, the more cliffhangers, the better, and the earlier you are in the relationship, the more you'll need to offer them. You might want one big business-oriented tentpole cliffhanger that everything else can connect to. That ensures *something* is going to happen.

Then, with that set up, you can offer lots of little helpful things, like connections to other partners, thought pieces you can send over, or a link to that great restaurant in the city they're headed to soon. You get relationship bonus points for things outside what you're paid to do. A nice mix of potential paid and unpaid follow-ups is best because it shows you care as an expert advisor and as a human being.

The Best Wording for Recommendations

How you word recommendations makes all the difference. We already talked about "Would it be helpful if...?"

If you need more oomph, I offer you two ways to word a recommendation. They lean on two of the six levers of influence we talked about in the last chapter: Authority and Social Proof. Here they are, with examples:

Authority-based recommendation:
"This has been an engaging conversation. Based on my experience, I'd recommend we _____."

Notice that version puts the power in *you* because you're the authority, with you giving your expert recommendation.

Social Proof-based recommendation:
"This has been a great discussion, with many similarities to what we've seen with other organizations like yours. What most of our clients do next is _____."

Notice that places the power in *others*, specifically your clients, instead of you. All the cool kids are doing it!

Read the room to realize which will work best, but here's an easy decision tree to use most of the time. Use the

Authority option for people and cultures that have a top-down approach. It's more forceful and works best when it's normal for the client to take their orders from above. Use the Social Proof option for people and cultures that are more collaborative. It's softer and works best when it's normal for clients to seek lots of people's input before moving forward.

Both can work great, and you can choose which to use based on what will help the client the most. Some want the authority figure to tell them what to do. Others want to do what others do.

However you phrase it, use your words. Say it out loud. Build in the time, cut through the clutter, and tell the client what's next. If you find yourself hesitating, remember you can't make the impact you want unless the client takes the next step with you. And you don't want others to be confused, which leads to inaction, or to make the wrong choice—you need to recommend what that next step is.

After you make the recommendation, you want to transition to see what the client thinks, then enter into a mutually beneficial discussion.

Pro Tip: Spend as much time finalizing and practicing your recommendation as you do finalizing and practicing the content you'll share. Most professionals treat the recommendation as an afterthought, secondary to the other insights they'll share. I don't recommend this! Work with your team on what recommendation you'll likely give. Practice it. Think through all the prospect's possible reactions. Decode what each person wants out of this topic and how they'll likely react.

Practicing your recommendation is just as important as practicing the main content you'll cover.

Your recommendation is where all the leverage is, so you'll want to get it right and anticipate every permutation of the conversation after you give it. Bonus: practicing your recommendation and what will happen afterwards will give you more confidence, too.

How to Lead the Post-Recommendation Discussion

OK, let's say you've made your recommendation. You had the confidence to say it and say it clearly. They're about to respond. Heart thumping, blood pumping, you think, "I want the yes."

Record scratch. Rethink that!

When talking through your recommendation with the client, you actually don't want the yes. You want the truth.

Here's why: You don't want to push anyone to a short-term yes. A short-term yes can lead to what we call the Slow No. That's a coerced yes in the short term that never goes anywhere in the long term. Slow Nos are the worst.

I'm sure you've experienced a Slow No before. The meeting seemed to go well. You enticed the client to say yes to what's next. You tell your boss about the opportunity. Maybe others. Expectations mount. Then... nothing. For weeks. Then months. The Slow No will kill your momentum not just for that pursuit but also for others because it seeds doubt in your mind. (Look out—here come the lies!)

That's why you want the truth. You're influential, so pushing someone to a yes in the short term can disguise a Slow No in the longer term.

So, if there's a no, you want to know it as soon as possible.

Pro Tip: Buckle up, because what I'm about to recommend is controversial, but I recommend it, and a lot of people use it. I usually like ending the recommendation with this: *Does that sound good to you, or not?*

The controversial part of that is the "or not" at the end, but those two words carry a lot of weight. By ending the sentence with a negative, those that aren't interested will tell you. And those that *are* interested will swing to the ultra-positive: "Oh no, this sounds really interesting. How would that work?" You don't have to use that phrase. I don't use it every time; I use it when I'm unsure of what they're thinking or my recommendation is on the bolder side.

Whether you use the "or not" or not, make it easy for the client to say no. By doing so, you'll avoid what we call "happy ears," a mindset where you want the yes so bad you can't hear the implied no. I promise you this: having happy ears in the moment will make your entire self sad in the end. Here's what to keep in mind:

You want the client to make a decision. A fast yes is great. A fast no is great. Above all else, avoid the Slow No.

Here's the mindset you should have instead of happy ears:

After you give your recommendation, be passionately agnostic.

Be passionate that your recommendation is the right one and that you can help the client. Be passionate that you can make an impact, that you'll exceed expectations, that everyone will win. And at the exact same time...

Be agnostic as to whether they take you up on your recommendation. They might not have the capacity themselves. They might have other more urgent priorities. Their budgets might be frozen. Their team might be going through a tough transition. Being agnostic will also convey that you're in demand with other work (creating scarcity!) and make it clear you want the truth.

Striking this balance can be difficult, especially if you feel pressure to close the deal. But just remember, we're optimizing for both the long-term relationship and the investment of your time. The client will appreciate you're not being pushy, helping the long-term relationship, and you'll appreciate getting the truth, helping avoid Slow Nos!

Here's the best part: being passionately agnostic is attractive. The science is called the "but you are free" approach, or what scientists call the BYAF technique.

BYAF is widely studied, and when something's widely studied, someone does a meta-analysis studying all the studies. Researcher Christopher Carpenter and his team did just that. Here's the abstract of their meta-study, summarizing the BYAF approach and their findings (italics added by me for emphasis):

> *The "but you are free" (BYAF) compliance-gaining technique operates by telling the target that he or she is free to refuse the request.* A meta-analysis of 42 studies of the effectiveness of that technique indicated that it was an effective means of increasing compliance rates in most contexts. It was effective regardless of type of request, *but effectiveness diminished when the decision to enact the target behavior was not made immediately,* consistent with a self-presentation explanation of the technique's effectiveness.

So interesting! Two takeaways will help you dig deeper: 1) you should subtly mention it's OK for someone to decline your recommendation; and 2) you want to make a recommendation *in the meeting you're in*. If you don't, you lose time and the 34x superpower of an in-person ask, and your BYAF powers diminish quickly too. This is why...

The fastest path to a yes is making it clear someone doesn't have to say yes.

BYAF taught me something broader too. Using soft language shows your strength.

Let's close out this chapter by taking things up a notch: ask for escalating commitments.

Ask for Escalating Commitments

Some people call this "qualifying," but I don't love that concept. That has too much of a short-term mindset for me. Our perspective is long-term relationships, so people will naturally fade in and out of being "qualified" over time. I prefer the words "interested" or "motivated."

Buying something big needs client interest and motivation. Because you're likely investing in their success with Give to Gets, you need an easy way to test if they're truly interested in hiring you later on or if they're simply fired up about getting your free stuff.

You are escalating your commitment by investing in their success, so why shouldn't they invest a little? It's fair they should escalate their commitment too. And you need a way to gauge their interest—the best way to do that is to ask for an escalating commitment on their side and see how willing they are to make it.

Here are the top three escalating commitments to ask for:

1. **They invest money.** This is the best sign of commitment. Even if it's not a huge amount, you'll know they're serious if they're willing to pay for the next step.

2. **They invest time.** The next best thing to them investing money is them investing their time. My favorite way for them to invest time is if they'll co-create a proposal. Maybe they collect and scrub a lot of data to send to you. Maybe they review something like a sample contract, project plan, or other work product. Whatever it is, they'll show you their interest and motivation if they invest some time before your next cliffhanger meeting.

3. **They invest social capital.** While this is the least powerful, it's still powerful. Here, they're putting their name on the line. Maybe they set up executive interviews or focus groups. Maybe they pull in some broader decision-makers to meet you. You'll know someone is serious when they spend social capital to advance your collective cause.

Pro Tip: Co-creating proposals is exceptionally powerful. They're a surefire way to gauge interest, and it'll result in a process that leverages the IKEA Effect. The math is moving: you spending two hours co-creating a proposal with a client is better than you and your team spending two hundred hours creating one without them. Even if you do write the perfect proposal, the only way your client can add value is by poking at it. Let them shape the approach whenever you can, to the extent you can. It'll take less time and have more success.

Back to the three escalating commitments. Any of the three can work great. Build in an escalating commitment into your recommendation. Share what you'll do and ask them to do something too. If they jump at it, great! If they hem and haw, showing a lack of commitment, then that's great too.

Either way, an escalating commitment will show you the truth. Actions speak louder than words, so ask them to act. You'll find out if they're really engaged by their response, and you can decide how much to keep investing after you know the truth.

Let's close this out with a conversation about closing. I often get asked to talk to someone who surfaces a lot of opportunities but has trouble closing, like closing is some magical skill that only happens at the end of a buying process.

Closing happens in small, safe steps with escalating commitments throughout the buying process, not as some big magical leap at the end.

Someone not good at closing is someone not good at asking for escalating commitments.

The escalating commitments I can recommend are...

1.

2.

Asking for escalating commitments gives you information about intent to buy. Sometimes it'll make sense to invest when there's nothing the other person can buy. That's investing in the relationship. Do that and do it often. It's awesome. Just don't think you're going to land a major opportunity when you're just investing in the relationship.

It's different when there's something the client should buy from you in a way you can help them. That's when you should make recommendations and test their intent to engage in the next step. Asking for escalating commitments will do just that.

It fits to end this chapter with a recommendation, and this is one of my strongest in the book. Make recommendations. *Always*.

I've trained tens of thousands of professionals, and it's the number one thing you can do that speeds things up. It's what all of the Top Performers I've seen do, and they do it consistently.

But here's the thing: you're free to not do it. You're free to let the client be confused and wondering what to do, with their confusion leading to them doing nothing. And you're free to get more Slow Nos. Your ears will be happy, but your clients won't be.

And you're also free to speed things up with cliffhangers your clients will love and look forward to so you can make a bigger impact and get the yes faster. It gives them the Gifts of Clarity and Progress.

With that as a final recommendation, I've got one last question.

Does that sound good to you, or not?

Section Four:
The Impact

Transition time. This last section is going to focus on the actions you'll take and the impact you'll make.

I'll break down your actions into three parts: succeeding in the moment, succeeding in the short term, and succeeding in the long term. All three will cover both the mindsets and moves you'll need to succeed, covering everything from mentally managing the random roadblocks you'll experience to the routines you'll run, plugging them into your calendar to stay on track.

Throughout this, we'll show the impact you can make— not just on clients, but on everyone around you.

If you get your mindset and moves right, you'll make the impact you want.

And from doing this a long time, my bet is you can make a much bigger impact than you think.

Chapter 16

Succeed in the Moment

I'm going to get real and raw for a second.

Almost everything in your daily life is going to try to distract you from deepening relationships.

The lies will try to creep back in your head.

I can't.
I don't know how.
I might do it wrong.
I'm too busy.
I might look bad.

We can't help our friends, our colleagues, or clients with the lies that are lying to us.

Top Performers prioritize people. They raise up relationships. And they find ways to do so no matter what comes their way.

Your success will directly correlate to how quickly you can adapt to changing situations mostly outside of your control and take action in ways you can control.

Here are some examples. Most people slow down after they get good news because they're ahead of their expectations. Top Performers use good news to *speed up* relationship development. Most people quit after they get bad news because they assume things weren't meant to be. Top Performers know people bond in times of stress and use bad news to *deepen* relationships.

In this chapter, I'll show you how to take whatever broader news you get and transform it into positive action. You want to be able to do this quickly, because faster transitions translate to faster results.

Good or bad news, fast or slow progress, it's always your move. And the move is always to deepen the relationship.

But before we emphasize the positive, we need to recognize the negative.

Bad Is Stronger than Good

You already know that bad is stronger than good. Look at all the lies we covered. A little lie can go a long way in slowing your success. But the science is deeper than most think.

All-star researcher Roy Baumeister and his team led a meta-study on the impact of bad. And in nearly every domain, bad is stronger than good. The results were so strong they named their paper exactly that! Here's the bad news in their study on bad:

> The greater power of bad events over good ones is found in everyday events, major life events (e.g., trauma), close relationship outcomes, social network patterns, interpersonal interactions, and learning processes. Bad emotions, bad parents, and bad feedback have more impact than good ones, and bad information is processed more thoroughly than good....Hardly any exceptions (indicating greater power of good) can be found. Taken together, these findings suggest that bad is stronger than good, as a general principle across a broad range of psychological phenomena.

Bad is stronger, faster moving, and more resilient than good. But don't worry about this parade of horrible. By seeing and anticipating bad's immense impact on us, we can better handle it. First, the facts.

Bad news will impact us harder, hit faster, and stick around longer than we think.

Now, think about the Doing the Work versus Winning the Work table in Chapter 3. We're used to near-perfect successes when Doing the Work, getting much less bad news than when Winning the Work. I mean, sure, things go wrong, but *much* less wrong and less often when we're Doing the Work. This amplifies the bad news and setbacks when we're Winning the Work because we've trained ourselves with Doing the Work expectations.

All of this is why we need a special mindset to succeed in the moment.

The faster we can recognize we're being negatively impacted by negative news, the faster we can act positively.

Here's what you need to know next.

Detach Yourself from the Outcome You Want

Your bank account statement wants the bonus, originations, or revenue credits. Your ego wants the recognition. Your competitive nature wants the win. You want the outcome, but you can't control the outcome.

The more you fixate on something you can't control, the more likely you'll slow down and get stuck.

That's why you have to detach yourself from the outcome and attach yourself to your next action.

Author and alternative medicine advocate Deepak Chopra has the best overview of detachment I've seen. Here's a shortened overview from his book *The Seven Spiritual Laws of Success*:

> Only from detached involvement can one have joy and laughter. Then the symbols of wealth are created spontaneously and effortlessly....Without detachment we feel we must force solutions onto problems; with detachment, we are free to witness the perfect solutions that spontaneously emerge from chaos.

Viktor Frankl says it more succinctly in *Man's Search for Meaning*:

> We have absolutely no control over what happens to us in life, but what we have paramount control over is how we respond to those events.

Those are deep ideas, so let's make them practical. Here's how to use them to guide you.

You Have Agency No Matter What Happens

Let's start with one thing we've covered and build on it.

It's always your move.

That's the ultimate shortcut to remember. You have agency!

You can always reach out and check in. You can always make another offer of help. You can always build another way to be of service. You can always react to something in a way that helps your future self and everyone around you.

Your view on what's going on is important. You'll view news as bad if it makes the outcome you want more unlikely. And you'll view news as good if it makes the outcome you want more likely.

Don't blow in the winds of what you can't control. Always keep this in mind.

It's always a chance to deepen the relationship.

I'll underscore one word: always. It's *always* a chance to deepen the relationship.

Good news happens? Don't slow down; speed up. Offer something new and of more value. A little extra. Delight and surprise.

Bad news happens? Realize people bond in stressful times. Offer something that debriefs the situation, digging deeper. Find ways to truly understand what's happening. Then find another way to help.

And what if no news or no response happens at all? This is just a subset of bad news; it usually happens because the value wasn't large enough or communicated in a way that resonated. Find another path to add more precise value.

Detach yourself from the outcome you want. Don't view the short-term news as the final answer. Combining our thoughts with even more emphasis...

It's *always* your move, and it's *always* a chance to deepen the relationship.

Next up, I'll show you the top scenarios we see, along with how to handle each one. Some of these are viewed as bad, some good. Some are felt deeply, others on the surface.

No matter what, notice the themes. You have agency and are in control. You can turn things around or accelerate your momentum. Some don't see their agency at all, and many others don't see it as soon as they should.

Do what you need to do to feel agency immediately and act on it right away.

Top Performers make quick mental transitions. They feel all the things everyone else does, but they make faster transitions to act with agency. Whether they feel something is good or bad, they swiftly move from feelings to positive action, always moving forward.

And more deeply, they don't connect the latest news with their identity. One client responding or not responding to you doesn't mean you are or aren't helpful and valuable. You're helpful and valuable if you're consistently helpful and valuable. So don't let the moments *become* you one by one. Let your ongoing actions become you.

James Clear[8] has a great line in his book *Atomic Habits*: "Every action you take is a vote for the type of person you wish to become." You have agency. You are in control.

Notice everything significant that happens to you. Observe your reaction. Then move to positive action in a way that deepens relationships.

Respond to frustration with generosity. Respond to rejection with generosity. Respond to setbacks with generosity. Respond to everything with generosity. Do this over and over.

Quick mental transitions create more positive actions that drive faster and bigger results. The big doesn't eat the small. The fast eats the slow.

Here are some examples to help you visualize what to do.

---

8 When James was on *Real Relationships, Real Revenue,* we used his *Atomic Habits* framework to solve the top problems I see our audience struggle with. So good! See givetogrow.info for a link.

Example Moves That Succeed in the Moment

You Get an Introduction

Bam! These are more important than they appear, because the strongest thing someone can do for you is recommend you.

Most people focus on the person they're being introduced to, but I'd recommend spending just as much time on the person making the introduction.

Ask: What can I do to inspire confidence that the introducer should introduce me again? You want to overcommunicate with the introducer throughout the process. Let them know you're thankful for their introduction. Let them know when the initial conversation occurs and share whatever helpful impact you had on their friend.

This is, by far, the top thing you can do to get more introductions. If they know their introduction made a positive impact, they'll make more of them, and it'll deepen your relationship every time they do.

You're in the Middle of an Introductory Meeting

Let's say you started a first-time meeting with a prospect, and you set up the beginning frame nicely. After that, it can sometimes be hard to tell if it's going well or not, and your feelings can take over. They'll be based on some invented progress bar in your mind telling you whether you're on track or not. Vacillating back and forth, your mind is in overdrive, stressing you out and stealing your focus.

This kind of thinking can be debilitating.

Detach yourself from the outcome and focus on engagement. What question should you ask next? What do you need to learn to test your understanding of their priorities in their own words? Once you know that, what offers of helpfulness can you make that leverage your knowledge and network?

Focus on finding the Give to Gets to offer and figuring out what recommendation to make.

You can't control how they'll respond. You can't control if the time is right to work together. You can't control what offers will resonate. But you can control how you invest in their success. And if you do that well, you'll always be moving forward.

It's always a chance to deepen the relationship.

Someone Doesn't Respond to an Outreach

First, expect this will happen, and happen a lot. Expect nonresponses. Think 10x, not 1x—that you'll keep offering value ten times over a period of time and maybe get a response on one of them.

Even with that in mind, it can be easy to think of nonresponses as bad news, letting the lies creep in. A better way of thinking is this:

Sometimes you win, and sometimes you learn.

Focus on what you learned. Maybe they don't prefer this communication medium. Maybe the offer didn't resonate. Or the most probable answer is they're just busy.

Focus on your actions. Go again. Try a different offer or different communication medium. A nonresponse can be a great thing because it means your next try will mean more.

You guessed it. It's always a chance to deepen the relationship.

Someone Responds to an Outreach

Great news—someone responded!

Same drill: Use it to learn. Make a note on what resonated in your files. Respond with a 15 percent bid to deepen the relationship, either on the personal or professional side. Notice what they responded to. Then offer even more value.

In this situation, don't just be happy, *accelerate*. Not every response deserves a reply, but most do. Ask: What can I do to deepen the relationship? Then do that.

You Get a No for a Give to Get

Sometimes it's hard to get a yes, even for something that's free. No biggie. Staff demands, priorities, and lots of other things can get in the way.

Think of this positively. You got an answer. They made a decision. You avoided the Slow No.

There's some interesting science called "rejection then retreat," sometimes called the "door in the face" technique. The idea is that you have an outsized chance of getting a yes right after you get a no, especially if the secondary request is logically aligned with the first.

Ask: What offer can you make that is smaller but aligned with the no you just got? It can feel like a "No worries, but let's at least do ____" suggestion. Or can you deepen the relationship by offering a check-in call to better learn their priorities and offer a more valuable investment? Maybe an aligned but smaller Give to Get that's easier to implement? Something else?

You'll set yourself apart when you strive to continue to invest after a no. And you have an outsized chance of a yes if you do. It's hard to tell someone no, so the prospect's probably feeling a little bad about it.

Now's the perfect time to keep trying. You'll deepen the relationship by continuing to offer to invest.

You Get a Yes for a Give to Get

Great news—double down!

You know the mantra: this is a chance to deepen the relationship. What's one little extra you can offer right after the yes? Maybe including an even better expert? Adding a bit more to the analysis? Adding a pre- or post-session? Offering to share the results with a broader or higher-level audience? Investing in one of their high performers as you do the work?

Ask: What little bonus idea can I offer to what they're already excited about, personally or professionally?

We Have Someone for That

It happens. They already have someone. Guess what: this is a chance to deepen the relationship.

Other competitors would go away at this point, which shows they only cared about the prospect as a budgetary line item. The client expects that, so it's a low bar to clear to exceed their expectations. Leverage that. Where there's a hill, there's a way.

At this point, they're thinking they already have someone for a large piece of work, so it's best to go small. Offer a Give to Get on a narrow topic that plays to your strengths. Leverage the impact of "rejection then retreat"—you've got a short-term, outsized chance of a yes. Focus on finding a small, specific topic and build up from there. Maybe it's offering a market overview, a legislative update, a data analysis, an introduction to a helpful contact, or a quick second opinion.

The point is, don't just scurry off like you were a car salesman trying to put them in a car today. Instead, give. Continuing to try sends a strong signal about how great a partner you are. And by offering to invest in a small way, you're making it easy to say yes.

And if you get another firm no, they're not willing to escalate their commitment with time or social capital in the slightest? That's OK too. It's great they made a decision. Drop back to staying in light touch. You never know when your competition will falter, and you want to be next in line; focusing on the relationship in helpful ways will earn you that position.

You Lose Something Big

This is a special case, one worthy of a little more space. You wanted it but you didn't get it. You lost. You can't change the outcome, but you can...

Turn every loss into your next win.

First and foremost, ask for a debrief call. I'm shocked by how many people don't. Every client will engage in these, and they're the most valuable fifteen or twenty minutes you can have because of the magnitude of the situation. Try to get this in person, but at the very least have your camera on during a video call so you can see each other.

Here's a surefire format:

1. **Show gratitude.** Share how much you value them and that you want to learn from the experience because you're focused on the long-term relationship. Share that their time will help you serve them in the future.

2. **Learn.** Ask them who won and why. Even if they can't share specifics, you'll learn a ton about what mattered to them. Then get specific about your pursuit. Ask them for their advice, "What's one thing you would advise us to change about our approach next time? And what's one thing you would tell us to keep?" These questions provide insights because most clients will try to hide behind "there was nothing you could do" answers. There's always something you can do differently next time, and you want the client to tell you what it is.

3. **Strategize.** Shift to future topics and offer to invest in the relationship. You can't change the past, so you'll want to shift to the future. This step is a big relationship-deepening move. Say something along the lines of "Even though we didn't win, we want to invest in our relationship. Can you share a different priority where we might be able to invest in your success?"

4. Recap. End with next steps. Maybe you just decided on a Give to Get. Or maybe you'll check in after a few months or send info on a specific topic as it crosses your desk. Whatever it is, people love ending with agreed-upon next steps. That's progress!

Pro Tip: Sometimes steps 3 and 4 will surface a clear action you can start on right away, and sometimes they can be an "if this, then that" (IFTTT) action. IFTTT examples might be following up after their strategy finishes or sending them thought pieces on priority topics when you publish them. Anything works, but whatever it is, agree upon the next steps. Either specific or IFTTT next steps are fine because you'll be deepening the relationship and you'll have an agreed-upon reason to follow up.

I will remember to deepen the relationship by...

Focus on What You Can Control to Succeed in the Moment

No matter what happens, just remember:

There's always a way to deepen the relationship, and it's your job to find it. Doing this will separate you from the outcome you can't control and turn your focus to the winning move you can control.

To have the fastest transitions, fully feel the emotion of any news outside your control. Feel the lows and the highs. Don't try to control your emotions with logic, because that doesn't work—at all. Emotions are like a red indicator light going off, signaling you to pay attention, so don't ignore them.

Pro Tip: To fully process an emotion, science shows it can help to label it. Give your feeling a name. After naming it, I find that talking about it with someone using the label helps me process it right away. I just say, "I'm disappointed that _____ happened" or "I'm stressed because of _____." You won't be able to take the logical action until you process the emotion, so find a way that works for you. Then, as fast as you can, move to action.[9]

------

9 The best person I've ever seen do this is Henning Streubel of Boston Consulting Group. He outlined his approach in a podcast interview on *Real Relationships, Real Revenue*. Link at givetogrow.info.

Rapidly moving from emotion to action wins each moment. It's the fast path to success. Like a great athlete on the field, find ways to speed up your reaction time. Focus on how fast you can transition from new news or a new feeling to new action.

Think back to something I mentioned about Top Performers earlier in the book:

Top Performers make more attempts.

Say the average person in your organization makes one hundred offers to be helpful in a given time period. Top Performers make one thousand or more. Quick mental transitions, swiftly moving from news to action, is one way they do this. They reframe the setback as adventure. They act. They master the moments.

There's a Japanese proverb that says, "Fall down seven times, get up eight," and that summarizes what Top Performers do. They go again. And again.

I originally wrote this chapter as a fable showing the highs and lows of a multi-month pursuit. Early readers found it polarizing, with half saying it was the best and half saying it was the worst chapter of the book! I kept the early manuscript and am including it as a "secret chapter" you can download with the other goodies at givetogrow.info.

Moments are bigger than they appear. Moments become days in the short term. Days become weeks. And weeks become years in the long term. Separating yourself from the outcomes you want will separate you from your competition, because you'll always be taking action and they won't. Take more action than others and you'll progress faster than others. Turn every moment into momentum. It's as simple as that.

Mastering each moment will help your future self succeed—and when you do that, you'll help everyone around you succeed too.

Go again.

Chapter 17

Succeed in the Short Term

For the majority of my life, I never felt like I was enough. Or that I was doing enough. Or that I was being all I could be.

I'm not sure why this belief crept into my mind. Maybe it was growing up in a small Indiana town. Maybe it was that I didn't hit puberty until years after my peers did, weighing 90 pounds as a freshman in high school and 120 when I went to college. *Skinny.* Everyone called me that, and I hated it. I always felt *behind.* And that feeling just stuck with me into my mid-forties. Nothing I ever did was enough to catch up.

This feeling was compounded because I always see opportunity. I just love ideas; I'm energized by what's possible. I think of new ideas all the time, creating items on my lists way faster than I can take them off. So my to-do list was always growing. And yet again, it didn't feel like I was doing enough.

Here's what I realized:

The big important things in life are projects that never end.

Tiago Forte calls lifelong projects "areas" in his book *Building a Second Brain*, because they're ongoing pursuits.[10] The most important projects in life are the ones that never end. My big pursuits go beyond BIG, including everything I'm interested in, like staying in shape, ultimate frisbee, cooking outdoors, vacations, helping friends, and (my favorites) being a great dad and husband.

Even to this day, with everything I do, I can still feel like not much gets done. This feeling of "not enough" used to poke me on Fridays because that's when I'd wind down the week and plan for the next. The list! Every Friday there were countless things on the list that weren't done. Most Fridays the list was *longer* than the last week.

I had a breakthrough as I was finishing the Focus Course, a video-based training created by my friend Shawn Blanc that teaches you how to focus on what's most important. I realized things had to change. I needed a new system, a new way. So I finished the course by designing a new weekly rhythm that worked so well for me that we incorporated it into our full GrowBIG training system.

---

10 Tiago was on *Real Relationships, Real Revenue,* where we applied his *Building a Second Brain* database frameworks to business development so you can systematize your work. See givetogrow.info for the link.

It's called the MIT Process, with MIT standing for "Most Important Things." The MIT Process only takes about fifteen minutes, and it's by far the most important thing I do every week. It'll help you prioritize long-term investments, hold yourself accountable even when you get slammed, and make consistent progress toward your vision. Most importantly, it'll show you that you're doing enough, as it defines success for the week.

The only way you can feel good about the week is if you define a finish line before you start.

This requires writing things down or having an electronic system to define and track our progress. Our minds are *terrible* at managing complex things in our heads, and your growth activities are the most important area in your life to manage.

Here's how to do it with max efficiency, getting the biggest bang per minute.

Determine Your Top Relationships and Opportunities

Start with Focusing on the Right People

Your expertise is vitally important, but your overall future success will be capped by the quantity and quality of your relationships, so we start with them. To get going, you need a list of *who* is the most important.

You need a prioritized list of relationships because if you try to keep up with everyone, you'll keep up with no one.

OK, I don't literally mean no one, but you certainly won't keep up with the most important people. That's because of a mental heuristic called status quo bias, where we tend to keep doing the things we've been doing. For relationships, you'll tend to keep hanging out with who you've been hanging out with recently.

We call this list of most important relationships a Protemoi List. "Protemoi" is a Greek word without a direct English equivalent. I first learned it meant "first among equals," and then some fluent Greek speakers told me it means "first in order." Either way, I just love the concept. Write down your "first among equals" relationships. They'll be your first in order to invest in.

Pro Tips:

1. **First, design your perfect mix.** Think through the perfect portfolio of people. Start with those that can choose or recommend you for work, either clients, Strategic Partners, or your internal colleagues. Choose clients if you know exactly who you'd like to work with, and choose Strategic Partners if your work is more episodic, meaning you don't know who will need your help in the future. Choose internal colleagues if they're your best path to the work you want. Start with whatever balance you think will work best, knowing you can change it as you go.

2. **Next, choose how many.** Pick the optimal number of people to invest in. For most people, five to ten is plenty. If you have to keep up with lots of people to keep a full pipeline, you might need more, maybe twenty max. Your limiting factor is your time, so start with how many people you can invest in once a month.

3. **Finally, be future focused.** Try to make your list more aspirational. The best list blends people you know well with others that your year-from-now self would love to know. You might even have some people on the list you don't know yet.

OK, activity time—let's create your Protemoi List.

My Protemoi People are...

Write Down Your Opportunities

Relationships are your long-term game and the most important to focus on, but you'll also want to write down your opportunities. Your Opportunity List should cover each thing you need other people to say yes to. That would include paid work, for sure, but also broader things like speaking at a conference, getting chosen to write in a publication, or being introduced to a new client. Think of an opportunity as a growth activity you can shape but not fully control—someone else needs to agree to do it.

Pro Tip: Just documenting your opportunities in one place is a game changer, but try to be more strategic. Top Performers map their opportunities to short-term, medium-term, and long-term time frames. Short-term opportunities are things you're already discussing and proposing. Medium-term opportunities are natural extensions of what you're doing but haven't yet been discussed. And long-term opportunities are things that you see others need but have enough newness that you're starting without momentum, needing to create demand because they're not connected to any current initiatives.

Top Performers stratify their opportunities across short-, medium-, and long-term time frames for two reasons. First, it's the only way to know how strong your pipeline is over a wider period of time. And second, simply documenting them will make you more compelled to act on them.

The opportunities I want to get a yes for are...

Choose Three Big-Impact Activities Each Week

You've already got a leg up on your competition because you've written down your most important relationships and opportunities. Just doing that puts you in the top 75th percentile or so, but we're not done yet.

You want to *act*, making the right moves to advance your relationships and opportunities. But while you're juggling Doing the Work and Winning the Work, you can't do everything, so you'll be more successful if you focus on the MITs.

It's simple. Just choose three things at the beginning of the week that are your MITs. Write them down *and* schedule time on your calendar to do them. That's it!

It sounds simple, but here's the science on why it's so powerful:

- **Our brains think in weeks.** By the time we're a young child in grade school, we know what a Saturday morning and a Monday morning feel like. We can tap into that with the weekly MIT process.

- **Goal setting correlates to high performance.** Edwin Locke is one of the most famous researchers ever. He led a meta-study of 110 goal-setting studies, ultimately finding that goal setting correlated to high performance across almost every context. Choosing your MITs each week sets your goal.

- **Short-term goals have a particularly high impact.** Another Locke learning here! He and researcher Gary Latham found short-term goals specifically increase the chance the goal will be accomplished. Shorter time frames even correlate to higher satisfaction. Daily is too short and monthly is too long, so weekly wins.

- **Weekly rhythms leverage the power of "fresh starts."** Researcher Dai Hengchen and their team found that specific short cadences "demarcate the passage of time, creating many new mental accounting periods each year, which relegate past imperfections to a previous period, induce people to take a big-picture view of their lives, and thus motivate aspirational behaviors." This is the Fresh Start Effect at work! Only get two or three MITs done last week? No worries, you can go three-for-three next week.

- **Pseudo-set framing helps us accomplish more.** Scientists call creating "sets" of goals "pseudo-sets," and they're motivational. This is why athletes create sets of activities—the sets help them stay focused and accomplish more. Think of a weight lifter that does three sets of eight repetitions. Or a runner that does ten 400-meter repeats at the track. These sets create higher performance because the predefined set focuses extreme effort within a short spurt. You work harder in each one because it's clearly defined and short. John Barasz and his research team proved pseudo-sets correlate to higher performance. You'll find you get on a roll when you define your set of three MITs each week—focusing on your key three makes you want to do them well and keep going after they're done.

- **Rituals increase performance and decrease anxiety.** Alison Wood Brooks and her research team found that consistent rituals both increase performance and decrease anxiety. Bonus points to them for naming their study "Don't Stop Believing."

- **Three signals a streak.** Researchers Kurt Carlson and Suzanne Shu found that doing three things signals a streak. This is why we stop at three MITs. You can do more, but do your most important three first.

Wow, that's some significant science. Start your weekly MIT process and you'll start to feel momentum. Don't stop believing—hold on to that feeling!

Choose Your Time for Each and Every Week

Here's the last process step: choose a fifteen-minute block of time you'll do this in every week. I'm a Friday at 3 p.m. guy, but do whatever works for you. Some people like doing this over the weekend when work slows down; others choose to do it on a weekday morning. Some people even do it right before a meeting they have each week to review things with their boss. Whatever works for you.

The main thing is picking a time you can do *every* week. The consistency is important because that's what connects you to your weekly rhythm. In your second week and beyond, you'll add a review of how you did in the prior week before you choose your next week's MITs.

It's this simple:

1. Review and update your Protemoi and Opportunity Lists.
2. Review how you did the week before: zero, one, two, or three MITs done.
3. Choose the three MITs you need to do the upcoming week, leveraging the access and insights you have with the meetings you'll have. Remember to integrate development with delivery.

4. Document them in a way that nudges you. You'll tend to manifest what you write down and see, so writing your MITs on a sticky note and keeping it on your desk is simple and powerful.
5. Put the time you'll need to do them in your calendar when you can do them.

That's it!

Pro Tip: Stay consistent. After you do this for four to five weeks straight at the same day and time, you'll notice your subconscious starts choosing your MITs before you even start writing. That's when you know you're locked in.

Choose These MITs

Here's a bit more on *which* things to choose. Satisfy these three criteria that spell "BIG" when you pick your MITs:

1. **Big Impact.** Choose the three actions that will have the biggest impact next week, not the easy stuff. Your actions might scare you a little—if so, that's a good sign they're Big Impact.

2. **In Your Control.** Write these down so they are 100 percent in your control. Not "get a meeting with Craig" but "offer to see Craig when I'm in Park City."

This is so important—if you write your MITs so they're in your control, you'll hesitate less and do more. And you can get three for three every week!

3. **Growth Oriented.** You're not allowed to fool yourself and think, "If I do a great job in the client readout, I'll be in good shape to get hired again." That might be true, but I'm assuming other forces will push you to do a great job in the readout—like, say, your ego and desire to do great work. Your MITs have to be about advancing something new, not doing work that's already been won. I do want you to integrate Winning the Work with Doing the Work, so maybe you can ask for some kind of growth-oriented next step in that readout. That counts. And you'll likely be leveraging your in-person super powers. 34x!

Remember, you can do more than three MITs a week. I hope you do. Just do the three that fit the BIG criteria first.

The Perfect MIT Mindset

My friend Cyril Peupion is a world-renowned productivity guru.[11] He has a memorable metaphor that aligns to

---

11 If you guessed I've interviewed Cyril on *Real Relationships, Real Revenue*, you're right, and he rocked. Link at givetogrow.info.

the MIT process that he calls "General Time versus Soldier Time."

General Time is when you think strategically about what you want to do. The general in your mind is for priority setting. Soldier Time is for following orders the general gives, simply doing. The soldier doesn't question; the soldier just does.

I've found this valuable because the way we think in General Time is the opposite of how we think in Soldier Time. The worst is when you mix up general and soldier thinking in one session, so avoid this. If you try to think about what to do *and* try to do it in one session, you'll get stuck. It's a slog, a mental molasses. Separating them into two different time blocks unleashes your growth productivity. Your MIT time is General Time. It's for setting your top three growth priorities for the week.

Pro Tip: Put a few days between your General Time and Soldier Time. Doing that will let your subconscious start working on your tasks, so when you sit down to do them, you're parked downhill, making progress right away.

Next week's MITs are...

1.

2.

3.

Let's close this chapter with three things to keep in mind. These three things will keep you on track, always making progress toward your goals:

1. **Choose your MITs based on the highest long-term impact.** The rest of the world will try to push you into short-term thinking and immediate gratification. Leverage the MIT process to stay focused on what will pay off long term. Remember the power of compounding! Your MIT process is like dollar-cost averaging investments in your future self. Your investments will grow faster than you think.

2. **Flex your effort to fit your capacity.** It's OK to be busy, but always do three MITs. It's OK if they have to fit in fifteen minutes or fifteen hours. Flex up or down, but always make progress. If you can do more relationship tasks beyond your top three MITs, great! You can tick off a zillion relationship tasks, but do your top three first. That's success for the week. Everything else is a bonus.

3. **Stay consistent.** Success in almost everything important in life, from fitness and diet to relationships, is about doing a little bit all the time and staying consistent. Doing small amounts consistently is easier and will result in bigger outcomes than sporadic bursts of heroic efforts.

It's funny how simple success is: making consistent progress toward a longer-term goal. Succeeding in the short term means consistently advancing relationships and opportunities in a systematic way. Choose to be in control, and do it consistently.

Be the boss of your future. Be the general.

Chapter 18

Succeed in the Long Term

Through complete chance, I had one of the most fascinating experiences of my career as a young actuary in 1993.

I got to spend two days listening to the managing partner of a top law firm describe what long-term success looked like at his firm. A lot of people would have paid for that experience, but here he was, paying us, because their leadership team wanted me and my senior partner to create an eighty-plus-year financial forecasting model. *It opened my eyes to what success in the long term looks like.*

There I was, in my mid-twenties, listening to this sixty-year-old uber successful leader share the statistics of success by year and role, including what it takes to get to the next level and why most don't.

The numbers told a story. It took seven years to go from beginning associate to partner, with 40 percent attrition a year. A paltry 2.7 percent made it there. There were similar statistics to make the highest levels of equity partnership, with only a few making it to the top, which even back then was hitched to Winning the Work.

I pushed Lotus 1-2-3 to the limit with countless columns of growth, decrements, roles, partnership points, and probabilities. I loved every second of the experience, from his chain-smoking-filled commentary to the complex calculations. The spreadsheet was so complicated that I'd time my bathroom breaks to when I'd hit the F9 Calc key because it would take half an hour to run the numbers.

That project gave me three decades of experience in three months. I could see what success looked like over time without having to experience it myself. I heard one of the best Top Performers talk through why most don't make the major career transitions and what it takes for those that do.

That project seeded a desire in me to decode Top Performer success, something I've been focused on ever since. Since then I've worked with countless Top Performers, and the pace picked up since I started BIG. I've spent dinners with them and interviewed them on our *Real Relationships, Real Revenue* podcast. Some are great friends. I'm always curious about what they do that makes them successful, especially in the major career moves, because different stages require totally different ways of thinking.

Now I get to interact with countless Top Performers every year. I get to hear about their decades of progress in hours. And talking to so many of them makes me feel like I've lived multiple lifetimes.

This chapter summarizes how they think about their careers and achieve so much. Knowing this will let you visualize where you want to go in your career—and how to fast-track getting to where you want.

The Three Levels of Top Performance

Top Performers blast through three very distinct plateaus of growth. These three plateaus happen in every organization, but because it takes someone years or decades to climb to and through them, most people don't see them clearly.

I got a glimpse of this as I was building that eighty-plus-year pro forma back in 1993, and I've dug deeper into these every chance I've gotten since. So great news— I'll paint the long-term picture for you next.

Seeing these lets you steer your career. You can see where you're at and what it'll take to get to the next level. You're welcome!

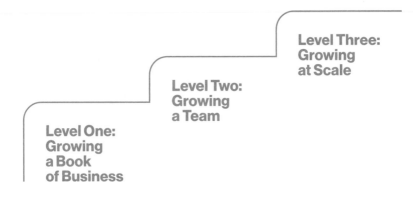

Level Three:
Growing
at Scale

Level Two:
Growing
a Team

Level One:
Growing
a Book
of Business

Level One:
Growing a Book of Business

Someone making it to Level One has built a solid, repeatable book of business large enough to earn their own keep. Some call this validation. Others call it equity partner or account executive. At this level you're bringing in far more business than what it costs to keep you; said another way, the organization can't afford to lose you. Congrats! You control your destiny.

This is a big deal. This person has made the transition from Doing the Work to Doing the Work and Winning the Work. Note this: the numbers can't be close. You don't want someone to have to create a spreadsheet to see you're bringing in far more business than it takes to pay you. It needs to be *obvious*. So make your personal growth goal multiples higher than what you're paid, including bonuses, benefits, and everything else.

Many people think the path to Top Performer ends here, but there are two more levels.

Level Two: Growing a Team

Someone at Level Two is now leading a team of people striving to be at or already at Level One. Think of the key difference here: this leader is now scaling their impact internally and externally. The three most common ways I see people scale are:

1. Bringing in so much business themselves they need a team of Level Ones to help win and deliver on the business
2. Helping others grow their business by coaching and mentoring
3. Scaling through some kind of systematized relationship development like effective Give to Gets used by their entire team

The best people leverage aspects of all three. Whatever the method, someone at Level Two is bringing up others to the point where they're valuable Level One performers.

Imagine how valuable someone at Level Two is! It's hard enough for someone to make the transition to Level One on their own. The Level Two person has created a *system* to help others rise up. If you've made it this far, you're invaluable. But there's one more level.

Level Three: Growing at Scale

This is the highest level because it scales indefinitely. The Top Performer making it to this level has added a new skill—finding and mentoring Level Two leaders with scalable systems.

This happens through the Top Performer employing several strategies:

1. Identifying and building brands around long-lasting high-growth market trends
2. Investing heavily in those high-growth areas while minimizing investments in stagnant or low-growth areas
3. Mentoring and recruiting above-average talent
4. Setting clear effort and outcome metrics for what it takes to be a part of the organization and only allowing people to stay if they hit them
5. Building systems to help people learn Winning the Work skills to the level the organization teaches Doing the Work skills

These Top Performers separate themselves when given more scale across a geography, solution, practice area, industry group, large client team, or other role that has many Level Two performers in them. And once you show you can do this at that level, the sky's the limit. You can run the entire organization.

Let's pop up a level and talk about the theme here:

What got you here won't get you there.

This is important—each stage requires learning brand-new skills. This leads us to...

Elite Top Performers don't stop when they build their own book of business.

Instead, they find ways to add even more value, first bringing individuals up to that level and then scaling that skill through teams.

They choose the role they want in the future, then identify the skills they need to be in that role, typically enlisting mentors and coaches so they can leverage deliberate practice, learning the skills as fast as possible.

Pro Tip: The fastest-climbing Top Performers start exemplifying many of the skills of the next level *while they're in the level before it*. This makes it obvious and safe to promote them because they're already doing parts of the job.

It's fine if you don't want to climb to Levels Two or Three. (Most organizations only require getting to Level One!) The more you love doing the work, the more you can steer your progress toward keeping more client responsibility. The more you love giving back to your organization, the more you can steer your progress toward internal leadership. Either is fine; you'll just want to be intentional about your path. You'll use the same skills either way.

Don't forget I mentioned back in Chapter 2 that we created a team implementation guide for *Give to Grow*. That'll help you scale your learnings across larger teams, helping you rise to or be effective at Levels Two and Three. Go to givetogrow.info to get it.

Top Performers use their Winning the Work skills both externally and internally, because the skills of positive influence are the same. The relationship work you'll do is the same too, whether it's external, internal, or a mix.

Now, let's think about where you want to be over the long term.

How to Get to Where You Want to Go: Cut to Climb

No matter where you're at, there's another level of impact. Even someone at Level Three has infinite upside. And because your limiting factor is your time, you'll want to focus on where you're investing it. I call this process Cut to Climb.

Envision your impact as a ladder, with higher on the ladder correlating to greater levels of positive influence and impact. What's one higher rung of impact for you? Is it working with bigger clients? Doing more of a certain type of work? Starting to mentor others? Building growth systems that scale?

Whatever it is, you're going to need time to do it. And because time is limited, you're going to need to cut something else out to get that time. Cut to Climb.

Before the steps, let me give you some science. You're set up to fail, to *not* do this well. That's because our brains are hardwired to add and not subtract. Researcher Leidy Klotz's book *Subtract* offers the best perspective on this I've seen.[12] In various experiments ranging from conceptual puzzles to physical tasks, participants almost

---

12 Yep! Leidy's been on *Real Relationships, Real Revenue* too, and he added a lot of value talking about subtracting. Link at givetogrow.info.

always solved problems by adding, not subtracting, even when the solution was faster and easier to reach by subtracting. We love to add. He surmised that the IKEA Effect was the reason—we love our own work so much that we're inclined to add things just to leave our own mark.

That's why you need to have a prompt to cut, to subtract. Let me say that another way:

Autopilot is your enemy. You have to remind yourself to subtract or you won't do it.

And the higher you go, the more important subtraction is. That's because you're busier and you'll get more opportunities offered to you. Looking backward, you need to remove to improve. And looking forward, you need a way of sifting through all the new ideas to discern what's worth testing versus distractions masquerading as opportunities.

Here's your Cut to Climb system:

1. **Schedule a recurring quarterly meeting with yourself or your team.** Think of how great athletes improve in the off season, which is their built-in time to repair, reflect, and strategize. You don't have built-in off seasons in business, so you have to build them in with a prompt. This is your off season,

and quarterly is the perfect cadence. Monthly comes too quickly and annually too infrequently. If the meeting is with yourself, thirty minutes is fine. You'll need longer with a larger team. Start with what you think will work—you can always tweak after the first go.

2. **Map out what you want to focus on in the next quarter and how long it will take.** Figure out what you want to focus on building, what the next rung is on your ladder of impact. Deeper relationships in that new division of a client? Strategic Partner relationships? Packaging up a Go-To Give to Get that'll scale? More mentoring? Whatever it is, choose what will take you or the team to the next level. Then create the next quarter's goal, defining what success looks like in that time period. Some of these initiatives might take much longer than a quarter to finish; if so, just break things down into a three-month burst. With that in mind, estimate how much time it'll take. Don't worry about precision. A guess is fine.

3. **Cut that amount of time from your existing responsibilities.** This is the part almost everyone misses. You need to figure out what to cut to be able to tackle the new priorities and climb. Take a look at your historical commitments, review what's the least valuable, and cut it out.

Pro Tip: You have to be *ruthless* in your cutting. It can come from any aspect of professional, personal, and volunteer time. You can totally eliminate things, automate as much as possible, or delegate some or all of a responsibility. Be as cold as you can be when you cut. Be creative about how to realign responsibilities. Involve others as needed. If you don't have agency over your time, no one else will. Remember what we learned from Adam Grant's research:

Successful Givers know how to say no so they don't get burned or burn out. Advocate for yourself: say yes to less.

That process is how the Top Performers keep climbing. That's why they can get to the 10x to 25x levels we talked about in Chapter 5. And beyond that, that's why this group transcends a singular book of business and moves to Levels Two and Three. They just keep cutting the least valuable things and building new skills to grow their impact. They're consistently winding down time spent on "good" activities to focus on what will take them to the next level. No wane, no gain.

I don't want to sugarcoat this. It sounds easy, but it's not easy at all. It's hard because things change as you transcend levels, requiring brand-new approaches. Here's the biggest reason most people don't keep climbing:

Ego is the biggest reason most people don't maximize their impact.

To maximize your impact, you'll need to trust others, even when you're marginally better at the task you're delegating. That's tough stuff, but it's better to have ten people doing something 80 percent as well as you do it, not only because the short-term throughput is over 8x better but also because in the long term they'll only improve if they practice the skill, and you'll be able to focus on higher priorities, blazing a trail to new capabilities.

I'll say it another way: in each transition, *you* are the limiting factor. It's the fight against your own ego, the fight against the lies that you're the only person that can do something or that you can do it faster, so you should.

Fight this! You'll never have an outsized impact if you let your ego win the battle of thinking too many things need to be done by you.

If you learned something, others can learn it too.

And if you don't have the right team now, you can find them. And even if you *are* faster doing the thing the very next time, it's not the best use of your time to do it the next ten times and beyond, which is what will happen.

Let me say it clearly. You have two levers to pull to become successful at Winning the Work: how much time you invest and how efficient each unit of time is. That's it.

Time first. You're uniquely suited to focus on the Winning the Work activities. Even if you build a great team around you, many of those activities have to be done by you or they won't happen at all.

Here's my personal, to-the-second example. I have the best team on the planet, but I'm the only person that can write this book, and I'll have about one thousand hours in the project the day we publish. That's half a work year!

To start the project, we had a series of meetings and countless calls handing off dozens of tasks and workflows I had been doing. It was *hard* to let go of these things, because I could do them at a high level while many were stretches for the team. It was a risk! But while it was hard to let go, the upside was that everyone else could rise up a rung of impact. Or three. If I stayed doing what I was doing, things would feel safe, but we wouldn't have unlocked the next-level upside this book will give us. Now that I'm finishing up the manuscript, I'm happy we did it. Everything's gone even better than I could have imagined.

Back to you. *You* are the first step. If you want to be successful, you've *got* to find ways to Cut to Climb, to shift as much as possible to others, even if that means taking some time to train them.

OK, that's the first lever: time. The second lever is the efficiency of each unit of time you invest. We've covered a lot of that already, like making quick mental transitions, prioritizing your actions with the MIT process, making more attempts, and so much more.

But you need to know one more thing to max out your efficiency, and it's how to think in bets.

Think in Bets: Think BIG, Start Small, Scale Up

Life's more like poker than chess.

Annie Duke is one of the most successful professional poker players of all time, and this quote is a full-on royal flush:

> You could teach someone the rules of poker in five minutes, put them at a table with a world champion player, deal a hand (or several), and the novice could beat the champion. That could never happen in chess.

Life's more like poker than chess because of randomness. In poker, you can have a great hand, bet it all, and lose. And a fool can win even with a bad hand.

But, over a full night of playing, let alone weekly poker nights over an entire year or decade, the skilled poker players will win over the unskilled, even with randomness thrown in. That's because they think in bets. You should do the same.

Don't let the randomness or luck in life lead you to the wrong conclusion that you don't have agency. *You have agency.* Focus on making the best bets and you'll get increasingly large returns. Time will smooth out the random things that will happen. Use randomness to your advantage. It'll slow down others, but you can use it to speed up because you can make the best decisions at the right times.

Top Performers think in bets.

Thinking in bets means three things:

1. Prioritize your investments based on your expected payoff.
2. Think big so you have high upside, but start small so you hedge your risks.
3. Double down only when something works, scaling up your investment with certainty.

We can summarize this with:

Think BIG, Start Small, Scale Up.

Let's dig into each one.

Think BIG

By Think BIG, I mean *choosing* the bets you'll make. You're in control.

You'll want to prioritize your investments based on the expected value of your payoff. Invest in the client that's the best fit. Invest in packaging up the Go-To Give to Get that's aligned with the high-value work you want. Invest in the Strategic Partner that has the platform of relationships best aligned with yours.

All of this gets you past the enemy of autopilot, which looks like continuing to do what you've been doing, but a touch better.

The new areas of focus for you will require some risk, so minimize it by choosing the ones that have the highest expected payoff.

Start Small

By Start Small, I mean *sizing* your bets to the perfect level.

You'll want to avoid jumping right into large investments, even if they seem like sure things.

Sometimes it makes sense to go full throttle right out of the gate, but it's rare. Let's say you were thinking of investing in a $1 million Give to Get because you were "sure" it would lead to a $20+ million program. That might be true, but what's the harm with starting with a half-day workshop to scope out the approach?

It's *really easy* for a client to say yes to your $1 million investment, but it's hard for you to know if they're actually interested if you start with the big offer. If the client says yes to the half-day workshop to map it out, they're at least committing *some* time, escalating their commitment and showing interest and motivation. Let's say you peg that they're genuinely interested at 80 percent, a pretty high number. That still leaves a 20 percent chance you wasted $1 million! You can start with the workshop to hedge your risk.

Personal sidebar: Almost every business mistake I've made is going too far, too fast, because I perceived something as a sure thing. I've wasted everything from fifty hours of my time to hundreds of thousands of dollars. Every time, in my Cut to Climb process, I realized I could've proposed something smaller to test the idea. Every single time.

Size your bets so they're modest when you're wrong and motivating when you're right.

You can always start small. Think you want to speak at a conference? Attend for a half day to see if the right people are attending and engaged, not hanging out in their rooms. Want to invest in a Strategic Partner? Test one mutual introduction first to see how it goes and make sure you're not dealing with a Taker. Want to invest in a Go-To Give to Get? Test the concept out with a friendly client using roughed-out materials before you make everything perfect.

Start small even when you're sure. It reduces risk. And funny enough, it will speed up your progress in the end if you slow things down in the beginning.

Scale Up

By Scale Up, I mean *focusing* your bets on what works best.

You'll want to double down when a bet pays off. Think of this like the opposite of King Midas. Don't put pressure on yourself to turn everything into gold. Instead, have a

Midas Mindset, testing what works and continuing to simply touch the gold you find.

Then keep making increasingly larger bets, expanding by 15 percent, similar to how we talked about deepening relationships. This is Give to Grow at its best—continually compounding just on the things that work. The fastest path is a slow ramp.

Have a Midas Mindset by touching things that are *already* gold. Double down on the bets that work and ditch the ones that don't.

Pro Tip: Manage your bets and investments like a broad investment portfolio. Not all of them will pay off in any year, but the right mix will pay off over a longer time horizon. And by reallocating your investments quarterly with the Cut to Climb process, you'll always have the optimal amount of time invested in the right bets.

And when things that were working stop working due to things outside your control like corporate mergers, changing marketplace trends, or shifting decision-makers and influencers, you'll be fine. You'll always have a growing list of people and opportunities compounding faster than anything that goes to zero.

Here's the best news. Just like a financial investment portfolio, things improve over time. The gains you make just keep getting bigger and faster because your relationship ecosystem gets stronger. You know more people and more *influential* people, and you've built the entire system on a foundation of trust.

Let's close this chapter with a provocative topic. This is counterintuitive at first, so give it a second to sink in:

The only way to be in control is to have more work than you can handle.

Having to make a choice about what to do is the best of all places to be in. It means you're valuable and you're in demand. You have options. Remember our phrase "the best time to sell is when you're sold out"?

There's an analog to your career: the best way to gain control is to have more work than you can handle. It's only then that you'll get the resources you need from your organization. It's only then that you get to choose the work you want to do. And it's only then that you get to choose the clients you want to work with.

Your long-term success will come down to just a handful of meta-skills: →

1. **Intentionality.** Be intentional about where you're headed next in the three levels.

2. **Practicality.** Break down the relationships and opportunities you need to climb to the next rung of impact, then identify where you need to invest next to get there.

3. **Focus.** Cut whatever your least valuable time investment is, even if it's something that's been successful, so you can focus on your next rung of impact.

4. **Consistency.** Do this over and over, never stop, and always strive for more leverage of your investments and time.

And as you win more, you get more control. You get to hire more resources, train more people, and do more of the work you want with the clients you want.

Let's close with some fun math. (Which is *obvious*, because of course math = fun!)

Remember that 15 percent compounding quarterly equals about 75 percent growth a year. It's shocking, but that same rate at the same quarterly compounding grows to 10x in around four years.

Being on autopilot will get you what you got before but a touch better: slow linear growth and about the same impact.

But instead, let's say you improve at a compounding rate. You think in bets. You Cut to Climb. You escalate your impact by Thinking BIG, Starting Small, and Scaling Up. You keep elevating your skills and impact with compounding results. That looks more like 10x in four years.

Some say slow and steady wins the race. I disagree.

Slow and *strategic* wins the race.

Chapter 19

This Is Bigger than You Think

"Mo! Mo! Mo!"

I was walking down a rainy street in Lisbon when I heard my name. It was Francisco, one of my favorite clients ever, and it was pretty clear he had something to tell me. We were both at his firm's big global meeting, with me speaking and him attending as a partner, and I was heading back to my hotel after leading some sessions. With a big smile, I turned to shake hands and hear what he had to say. I was curious, that's for sure.

A few years before, Francisco was selected for the very first GrowBIG training cohort at his firm. All the participants had to apply, so getting selected was a big deal. I taught that class and was excited to be there because of the firm's prestige and how much work we had put into designing the program. I was beyond excited for Francisco to be there because I had known him socially and always enjoyed his big ideas and quick wit.

I knew he had struggled with business development before the class started, feeling the pressure to bring in business but not knowing how to do it. I remembered him telling me a specific story of when he tried to get advice from a senior partner, and all the person was able to tell him was to "treat clients to great dinners." I could see my younger self in Francisco and remembered the fear I felt when I wanted a playbook and all I got was "treat the client right." We had a lot in common.

When the class started, everyone shared what they wanted to get out of the multi-month program. Francisco was the most honest. He shared that he had never brought in any business on his own, and despite him being a deep, functional expert in high demand, he knew that wouldn't get him where he wanted to be. He knew continuing to stay busy in his domain was a trap, but he didn't know how to get out of it.

We had a super session that day and followed it up with small group application coaching. Over several months, our team and client orchestrated an amazing experience for the entire group. The eighteen people in the program brought in over $20 million in accretive revenue in about nine months. So cool!

It was a great result, but the most meaningful win for me came months later on that rainy night in Lisbon. Francisco was happy to see me, ready to share. It turns out that he had been meaning to email me for a while, so it was fortunate we ran into each other.

He beamed as he updated me. By focusing on all he learned, he brought in over $10 million in revenue the year following our program, and none of it was associated with his functional expertise. He told me stories of working with senior C-level leaders to create new upside possibilities for them, and how they chose Francisco because he had engaged them throughout the buying process.

Even better, he got promoted to manage one of his firm's offices, so he could help train and impact the future generations of talent in a way he wished he would have gotten. Yet again, I could see my younger self in Francisco. I barely slept that night, thrilled with his success.

Francisco and I kept in better touch after that day, and we caught up as I was finishing up *Give to Grow*. He had just been in Argentina visiting his seventy-two-year-old mother, staying in the small condo where he grew up.

The visit unveiled some sad truths. His mom was having a hard time getting around. The condo was situated in a way that wasn't safe for her to load and unload basic things like groceries, including a series of steps that were becoming scary for her to climb.

As he helped her struggle up the steps, Francisco got scared. What if she fell? He remembered how she had gone into debt to buy the unit when Francisco was young just so he could be close to his school and around his friends. Her sacrifice was now a burden—not just financially, but physically.

After unpacking the groceries, he asked how she was getting around when someone wasn't there to help her like he did that day. She broke down. The truth was sinking in. It had gotten bad and was getting worse, and she didn't know what to do. It would take a lifetime to save up for a better home, and she didn't have it.

Francisco jumped into action, sharing his emotions. "Mom, I'm going to take care of this for you. We'll buy you a new home, one that you can get around in and be closer to your friends. I've got you."

I felt the tears well up in my own eyes as he described how they streamed down his mom's cheeks. She couldn't believe it. He had created a possibility beyond anything she could imagine. She was shocked. She was thankful. But most of all, she was proud. Proud of her son being able to help her in a way that didn't even seem possible.

Francisco could never have foreseen this scenario, but he was happy to channel his financial success into helping his mom. His act of kindness instantly transformed her life. At that moment, Francisco was superhuman. He made an impact on someone he cared about far beyond anything he ever could have imagined at the beginning of our class. And *that* is what everyone underestimates.

There's no doubt you'll see how this book applies to you because you'll improve your relationship and growth skills. You'll have more control. You'll be able to choose the work you want to do for the clients you want to do it for. You'll be winning.

But that's not the biggest impact you'll have.

The biggest impact you'll have is helping others win.

This is about much more than you. Walk through this exercise with me, measuring the impact you can have. Just jot down the numbers; I'll guide you through.

Think for a moment about your teams. If you're doing the work you want for the clients you want, you're feeding your teams the meaty work they'll be excited about. Whether that's tens or hundreds of people, bringing in the work you want impacts others. How many people in your organization can you impact if you get even greater at growth? Write down that number.

Now, think of your partners and peers. If you're on the forefront of bringing in "wow"-level work, they're engaged. Big-impact work is done by big teams, so you're helping them have an impact too. Maybe you help feed another ten or a hundred people. Write down that number.

Now, think of your Strategic Partners. Those people you admire outside of your organization are impacted too. And not just the tippy-top people you interface with, but their entire teams. Thinking through the ecosystem of other experts, tech providers, and others you influence can be invisible until you document it. Write down that number.

And it gets even better.

Now, think about your clients. The people you work so hard to positively impact. For most of the people we train, this impact is staggering. Your expertise doesn't just impact the people you interface with day to day, it helps both them and broad swaths of their organization. Do you do M&A transactions, HR policies, or product patents? *You're impacting entire organizations.* Write down the number—just a ballpark—of the people at your clients you impact a year.

Add all those up. Most of our clients get to thousands, tens of thousands, or hundreds of thousands in a flash. Your ripples of influence are bigger than you think. And it gets even bigger.

We know from research by Lieke ten Brummelhuis that when people are fulfilled and enriched at work, they are at home as well. Healthy at work, healthy at home. Your kids see you excited at the dinner table. Your spouse or partner is happy when you're happy. And you know who's most proud? Your parents. Doing great things makes them feel great. Here, don't add a number this time. *Write down their names.*

These are the people you care about the most. And doing great at work will help you do great work at home.

The scale of your impact is far bigger than you realize. And the depth of impact on those you care about is deeper than you can imagine.

Let me close the book with looking forward. My wife, Becky, and I often play a little game at night as we debrief each day. We always talk about the future, having fun predicting what will happen as we forecast someone's actions into expected future outcomes. We do it so much that the threads of the ongoing conversation build so we can decode what works and what doesn't. There's a lot of luck in life, so we're not always right, but two priorities have surfaced that work more than anything else, and both are in our control:

- Consistently investing in short-term actions that help our long-term selves
- Prioritizing relationships

The first bucket includes actions that grow in effect over time, like deepening our expertise, saving and investing money, and building systems you can leverage to get more done faster. Each small investment stacks, improves, and compounds with time, which makes each year easier, faster moving, and have better outcomes.

The second bucket is straightforward but hard to do. We spend a lot of time thinking through who we want to interact with, in what ways, and how we can be responsive when someone important to us needs our help.

The old saying "it's not what you know but who you know" doesn't give the whole picture. It's what you know *and* who you know. But there's more to it. The "what you know" part needs to include all the resources you can bring to bear: expertise, systems, and other helpful assets. You want to be able to add hours of value in minutes. And the "who you know" part isn't just knowing someone—it's *knowing* someone, meaning you've helped them immensely, you've built deep trust, and their life is meaningfully better off from having spent time with you.

The only other success factor beyond those two is luck. You can't control luck, but if you add immense value to a broad network of positive people, you expand the surface area and you can make your own luck. There's a ton we can't control, but I'm convinced we can impact luck a lot more than most realize.

Here's the problem. Almost every vector in the world will push you to focus on anything *but* those important priorities, enticing you toward short-term gratification with little long-term payoff. The weapons of mass distraction are attacking you every day. Social media. Unimportant but urgent emails. Clickbait headlines. Meetings where you aren't needed. The twenty-four-hour news cycle. Everything around you is trying to steal your attention. These activities don't stack, compound, or build trust with the right people.

So take control. Prioritize your actions. Focus on the right relationships. Say no to everything else so that you can *give*. And as you make these kinds of investments, you'll grow. And as you grow, you'll grow your ability to give even more.

Giving and growing connect and compound. They create a flywheel effect. *Momentum*. The more you use the skills in the book, the more you'll be able to use the skills in this book. And the more impact you'll have on everyone around you.

I'm proud to be a self-identified Otherish person, a Strategic Giver. I haven't always been as efficient as I should have been. Sometimes I've given too much and sometimes too little. Sometimes I've let the lies creep in my head, slowing me down.

But I've been consistent. I've consistently invested in myself and everyone important to me so we can all achieve what we want. And the results have compounded. Every week I answer a simple question in my own MIT process. I finish this prompt with whatever comes to mind: "This week, I'm grateful for..."

That answer has had a theme the last few years. I'm grateful for the growing set of tools and resources I have to help others, letting me add hours of value in minutes. I'm grateful for the remarkable people going above and beyond to help me help our clients succeed, including our clients helping other clients. And I'm grateful for this ongoing feeling I get that our ability to impact the world is accelerating, week over week over week.

Over and over, I'm overwhelmed by the support I get and the impact this community has on each other.

So welcome to this community that believes in what you do, that believes giving is the answer and growing means helping everyone around us. You're now part of a group making an outsized impact on the world and having a blast doing it.

Follow the mindset and methods in this book. Stay consistent. And...

Wake up every day helping your friends succeed.

Give to Grow.

You'll have a bigger impact than you could ever imagine.

Postscript: Look at All You've Learned

Remember how everyone reads a P.S.? You are right now!

Let's celebrate your progress, because we know how enjoyable that is. Here's the table we framed up in Chapter 3 about how the mindsets of Doing the Work are the exact opposite of Winning the Work.

We've tackled every one of them.

Here's the table again, showing the mindset or move we'll use for each (along with the chapter numbers where you can find each one).

	Doing the Work	Winning the Work
Clients respond	**always**	**rarely**
	See Chapter 11—Think 10x, not 1x, and disconnect yourself from the outcome	
Emails are	**long and offer clarity**	**short and offer help**
	See Chapters 6 & 8—Keep emails < 50 words and focus on Strategic Giving	
Communication is	**predictable and comfortable**	**fluid and uncomfortable**
	See Chapter 8—Make 15% bids	
You win with	**the best answers**	**the best questions**
	See Chapter 13—Design your questions to Fall in Love with Their Problem	
It's best to go in with	**a full presentation**	**a blank page**
	See Chapter 12—Focus on Engagement	

	Doing the Work	Winning the Work
You give away	**very little and manage to scope**	**as much as needed to create demand**
	See Chapter 14—Give Them the Experience of Working with You	
Feedback is	**quick and consistent**	**slow and irregular**
	See Chapter 15—Always Make a Recommendation	
Effort is rewarded	**immediately**	**in the future**
	See Chapter 18—Succeed in the Long Term (Levels One, Two, and Three) and Cut to Climb	

Doing the Work creates certainty for others.

Winning the Work creates possibility for others.

Wow, we've come a long way, solving for every single Doing the Work versus Winning the Work issue that exists. Dog-ear or somehow mark this page—you'll want to come back to it again and again. It's your IFTTT rubric for solving any problem you have, all in one table.

Time to celebrate!

P.P.S.

What's better than a postscript? A post-postscript!

Here's a killer idea to help you succeed with speed: *you can use this book to help yourself and help others.*

What could happen if your whole team was using the *Give to Grow* playbook? Or your entire organization? What about Strategic Partners *outside* your organization you often go to market with?

Give to Grow is powerful on its own, but it's even more powerful when scaled across a group. Working through all you've learned with a team will give everyone a deeply bonding experience, better ideas, leveraged strategies, better teamwork, improved action plans, and even shared accountability so everyone can keep making positive progress.

We've created powerful guides and systems to help you implement *Give to Grow* with your teams and partners.

And we've even got a secret backdoor way for you to order books in bulk at generous discounts.

Give to Grow is my legacy. It's my life's work, and I want to get it in as many hands as possible. I want *Give to Grow* to be the mantra of millions. And the only way that'll happen is if we scale.

Check out givetogrow.info to learn how we're making it easy to implement the system across a team.

This is my Give so you can Grow. I can't wait to see what we can all do together.

Secret Chapter

I originally wrote Chapter 16, Succeed in the Moment, as a fable, chronicling a consultant deepening a relationship with a potential client over a year-plus time period.

The story puts you right inside the protagonist's mindset of trying to be helpful while having to persevere and overcome all kinds of unexpected plot twists. It was my favorite chapter, and it was my wife Becky's favorite too, because it showed the challenges you have to overcome to make a big difference. I remember Becky saying, "I didn't realize how hard it is!" To me, it was raw, and there's real value in that.

But there was a problem. We created and sent about a hundred early reader prototypes of *Give to Grow* to close family and friends to get feedback and improvement ideas. That chapter was polarizing! Half the people loved it, and half the people mentioned it as their least favorite of the book. I didn't expect that.

So we rewrote Chapter 16 from scratch to convey the same messages in a way that was more consistent with the rest of *Give to Grow*. It was the right move, and I liked how it turned out. That said, now that you're finished with the entire book, it will be helpful to see the entirety of *Give to Grow* in a story. I kept that original version, and you can still get it at givetogrow.info.

Acknowledgments

So many people helped create this book that it's hard to think of them all. Our BIG community is big, including *so* many people that helped shape my thinking, create the space to write, refine the messaging, and help me bring *Give to Grow* into the world.

Let's start at the project level and broaden from there. Todd Sattersten at Bard Press has exceeded every expectation I've had. Bard Press only publishes one book a year, choosing the author as much as the author chooses them, and it shows. Todd and I have spent hundreds of hours messaging, calling, and digging deep in person. His thinking ripples throughout the book in deeper ways than I can describe. Todd is the *perfect babysitter* of the publishing world—you want to shout to everyone you found him, but for some reason you find yourself hesitating to do so because you want him all to yourself. Seriously, thank you, Todd. I had high expectations, and you've 10x'd them all.

My clients are next, and they're the best. Here's a little secret: because all our GrowBIG training is based on putting relationships first, we attract clients that put relationships first. If an organization wants normal (in the bad definition) "sales training," they choose someone else, and we're happy they do. So the hundreds of organizations we help are the ones with a relationship-centric approach already; we just help them accelerate their growth. What that means for me and BIG is we get to work with the smartest experts on the planet because *they* are a significant part of what's being purchased. Relationships matter to them because they matter to the people choosing them. For example, when Becky was in the hospital last year with pneumonia, our clients reached out as much as our closest friends did. Our clients are just the best there is. I've had countless clients shape my thinking, evolve a technique, tell me what's working, or just give me the emotional support I needed to write *Give to Grow*. It wouldn't be what it is without our clients, so if you're one of them, thank you! You've made a positive impact on me and it shows.

Next up, BIG. We have a bonkers-good team. Steve Jobs had a saying that "a small team of A+ players can run circles around a giant team of B and C players." I believe it's true, and that's what we've got. Darla Ward has been with us the longest and helped the most, so I need to single her out and thank her first. Thank you, Darla, you're my secret weapon! And to our whole team, thanks to all of you: Anna Boon, Mike Duffy, Anna Flurry, Maggie Glime, Ryan Grelecki, Bradley Humbles, Greg Humbles, Emma Jarrett, Gina King, Mary King, Marshall Seese, Jay Thompson, Lauren Titshaw, Alexa Ward, Ken Ward, and Paul Weigall.

Let's keep getting broader. Becky, my wife of over thirty years, is my model for giving. She runs a nonprofit called Reins of Hope that helps kids and breast cancer survivors through equine therapy. Those kids and women have faced undeserved headwinds, and I get to hear about her impact from them all the time. Sometimes it's through tears, sometimes it's through a heartfelt story, and it's always meaningful. Their situations keep us both grounded and provide inspiration far beyond the business world. But Becky inspires me well beyond that. Her constant caring for others flat-out flattens me. She checks in on her many friends. She keeps up with her ten brothers and sisters (seriously, ten). And she cares for our four horses, two cats, dog, and donkey all day, every day. (I keep up with the green-cheeked conure.) Becky's giving knows no bounds. Half of what I do is just try to keep up with her. Thank you for your inspiration, Becky. You make me better.

Then there are our two daughters, Gabby and Josie. Before we had kids I thought I'd be the one teaching them, but it's really the other way around. Both are so giving to everyone around them, including me. They both cheered me on, listening to my ideas as the book took shape, always telling me I could do it, and focusing me on all the people it would help. They kept me going. Thanks, G-Jabby and J-Gosie!

Let me finish my broad comments with my parents, Helen and John Bunnell. They taught me more about giving and growing than anyone. I watched them battle Dad's alcoholism, with his last drink on August 4, 1984. I watched them struggle to make a restaurant successful in a town of about a hundred people. And I watched them, through it all, stay married and flourish for over fifty years. They showed me what hard work looks like, what effect it has on those around you, and how focusing on relationships is always the winning move. I wouldn't be where I am today without you, Mom and Dad, and I thank you for everything you've given me, both known and unknown.

OK, now let's get super specific. So many people helped with granular elements of *Give to Grow*, and they all made a difference. I have so much gratitude to this group! Alan Wise taught me the opening saying in this book. John Hightower taught me the phrase "Think BIG, Start Small, Scale Up." Rod Garia provided inspiration in ways only he and I will know, which is our fun little secret. Tiago Forte taught me to properly document my second brain, so pulling from the hundreds of scientific studies I've documented was easy and enjoyable. Dian and Mike Deimler have added so many insights in Becky's and my life that their positivity and optimism ripples throughout the entire book. Michael Murphy, Craig Dolezal, and Andy Hiles taught me to fall in love with the client's problem. Kristy Ellmer taught me the simple phrase "go again." Josh Linkner exposed me to "fall down seven times, get up eight." And I have to mention *Ted Lasso*, which taught me about cliffhangers one night when Becky and I swore we wouldn't watch another episode but couldn't help ourselves.

A Bard Press Book

Publisher: Todd Sattersten
Operations Manager: Anne Ugarte
Text Design: Joy Panos Stauber and Richard Weaver, Stauber Brand Studio
Jacket Design: Joy Panos Stauber, Stauber Brand Studio
Copyediting: Sarah Currin, Wayne Woods
Proofreading: Katrina Taylor, Liz Wheeler

Early Readers: Lynn Bahnsen, Carla Bailey, Dennis Baltz, Jeff Berardi,
Anna Boon, Mason Brown, John Bunnell, Cannon Carr, Kayleen Duffy,
Mike Duffy, Mike Dulworth, Kristy Ellmer, Julia Fabris McBride,
Chris Fifis, Geoffrey Frost, Matthew Gartland, Scott Gaskill, Douglas Gibbs,
Evelyne Giguere, Marie Gill, Tom Gilmore, Tim Grahl, Bradley Humbles,
Greg Humbles, Josh Kaufman, Maria Kelly, Lisa Keyes, Gina King, Mike King,
Ray Kolls, Pete Lester, Mark K Lewis, Amy Looney, Mariana Loose,
Kelley Lugo, Missy McNabb, Ash Merchant, Debbie Muller, AprilJo Murphy,
Ed O'Malley, Ernesto Pagano, Jay Papasan, Nick Parker, Susan Paul,
Jack Phillips, Russ Richards, Tricia Schmidt, Amar Shah, Susan Slifer,
Jay Thompson, Keith Titshaw, Rose Ugarte-Gee, Kathryn Valentine,
Austin Ward, Jeff Ward, Eric Watkins, Paul Weigall, D.J. Whetter,
Troy White, Rob Whitfield, Scott Winter, and Damon Young

Copyright

Bard Press
info@bardpress.com www.bardpress.com

Ordering Information
For additional copies, contact your favorite bookstore or email info@bardpress.com. Quantity discounts are available.

First Printing—July 2024

Names: Bunnell, Mo, author.
Title: Give to grow : invest in relationships to build your business and your career / Mo Bunnell.
Description: Portland, Oregon : Bard Press, [2024] | Includes bibliographical references.
Identifiers: ISBN: 978-1-959472-10-0 (hardcover) | 978-1-959472-11-7 (ebook) | 978-1-959472-12-4 (audio)
Subjects: LCSH: Customer relations. | Business networks. | Business enterprises--Growth. | Selling. | Business communication. | Interpersonal relations. | Success in business. | BISAC: BUSINESS & ECONOMICS / Personal Success. | BUSINESS & ECONOMICS / Sales & Selling / General. | BUSINESS & ECONOMICS / Motivational.
Classification: LCC: HF5415.5 .B86 2024 | DDC: 658.812--dc23

About BIG

At Bunnell Idea Group, we help organizations and individuals Give to Grow in several ways:

- Custom Give to Grow workshops and keynotes, so you and your teams can apply the concepts in this book to your unique business and team
- Comprehensive GrowBIG training, so you and your team can learn *everything* everyone needs to grow, covering much more than we could in this book
- Higher-level GrowBIG leader training, so your leaders can scale growth strategies and mindsets across a larger team

We deploy all we do in every way possible, ranging from large keynote speeches to customized training programs to one-on-one coaching.

We can lead these in your location or connect virtually, whatever works best.

If you're curious about how we can collaborate, just reach out to info@bunnellideagroup.com and we'll set up an introduction.

You can guess what we'll do first: give!